How Self-Made Millionaires Build Their Fortunes

Also by the Author

How Self-Made Millionaires Build Their Fortunes

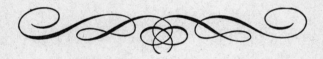

Scott Witt

Parker Publishing Company, Inc.
West Nyack, New York

© 1979 by

PARKER PUBLISHING COMPANY, INC.

West Nyack, New York

Library of Congress Cataloging in Publication Data

Witt, Scott
    How self-make millionaires build their fortunes.

    Includes index.
      1. Business.   2. Success.   3. Millionaires.
I. Title.
HF5386.W64   650'.12   78-31456

Printed in the United States of America

How This Book
Will Help You
Make a Fortune

You have in your hands the most authoritative guide to making a million dollars ever written.

Strong statement? Yes, but backed up by the fact that these pages give you, at a glance, the very techniques that took self-made millionaires years of trial and error to discover. Benefitting from their experience, you can progress rapidly with assurance that the moves you make are right. By learning what they did and how they did it—and how to use those same actions today—you'll have the best self-enrichment program ever devised.

The road to wealth can be far easier than most people realize. This book teaches you the most direct route and even introduces a few shortcuts. It follows the path cleared by scores of bootstrap millionaires who carved out their fortunes after finding the same techniques you are about to learn.

A STEP-BY-STEP PROGRAM
FOR BECOMING A MULTI-MILLIONAIRE

If one of the millionaires in this book were to write a thesis on how he or she did it, it couldn't be nearly as helpful to you as the volume you are now reading. That's because *you* are not that person, and some of the techniques he or she followed simply wouldn't work for you.

But, take the experiences of *scores* of self-made millionaires, learn which actions are for you and how to adapt them to your own abilities and circumstances, and you are well on the road to wealth. Like many of the millionaires you'll be meeting, this book lets you:

5

- Start from scratch, with little or no personal investment
- Follow a step-by-step blueprint that guarantees riches
- Attract wealth ideas like a magnet
- Learn new ways of making big money
- Utilize the secrets of self-made millionaires

It took many of them long periods of time to develop these million-dollar techniques, which now are yours for the reading. From their experiences you'll also learn:

- How to accumulate wealth-building formulas
- How to attract outside cash to your venture
- How to know in advance just how well you'll do
- How to let other people make you rich
- How to time your moves for maximum profit
- How to put experts at your command
- How to reap extra windfalls with little effort

A CHARTED COURSE TO MILLIONAIREHOOD

You will have something few wealth-builders have ever had before—your personal blueprint for wealth. It's personal because you'll compile it yourself following the instructions I give. It will be based on the millionaires' proven methods that *apply to you*.

You'll learn how to set your fortune goal (the bigger the better), how to mobilize the wealth-building powers you possess at this very instant, and how to acquire new talents for making big money.

Every step is spelled out for you, and every step is documented by the experience of people *who have already achieved the goals* you are now setting for yourself!

OPPORTUNITIES OTHERS NEVER DREAM OF

One of the most powerful techniques for building wealth is to take an existing product or service and make a small change that causes its value to skyrocket. Where others have failed, you *must* win! You'll see how this has been done time and again—and how you can do it.

Such "new twist" opportunities exist almost everywhere, but most people overlook them. I'll show you how to pick virtually any field and spot them right away. It can be done in such fields as:

- Mail order
- Retailing
- Food service
- Written materials
- Real estate
- Entertainment
- Construction
- Product development

The list is almost endless—once you know how to spot the special opportunities that I spell out for you.

HOW TO BE AN ACHIEVER INSTEAD OF A DREAMER

The best techniques in the world do little good unless they are converted into action. Most people dream their goals away. You're going to learn how to get going—immediately! The most important step in your step-by-step wealth-building program is the *first* step. Once it's taken, your drive to riches will virtually propel itself.

You'll learn how some of America's best known business people (their names are common household words) took their first steps and how you can make similar strides toward wealth.

IT DOESN'T TAKE MONEY TO MAKE MONEY

That is, it doesn't take *your* money to make money. You can start with zero cash, if you have no capital available, and still build a multi-million dollar fortune. Vast resources await you—outside investment capital just begging to be used. I'll lead you to it.

ENJOY LIFE AS A MILLIONAIRE

Anyone who wants to be rich *should* be, and this book proves that you *can* be! Others who dared to try succeeded, and like them, you can enjoy:

- Lifetime financial security
- Extended world travel
- Personal servants
- The thrill of helping others
- Luxurious homes
- Chauffer-driven limousines
- Security for your children
- The best health care
- Respect and admiration
- Control of a business empire

These and countless other benefits are being enjoyed at this very moment by thousands of self-made millionaires. What they have is your right to have as well. They exercised their right . . . now it's your turn.

NO BOOK LIKE THIS ONE

Never before has there been a book like the one you hold in your hands right now. Some give biographical sketches of millionaires, other give personal advice on earning money. But none has ever employed my own system of Compu-Analysis for digging out the precise methods that continuously make people rich.

My system:

(1) Computes the major moves taken by self-made millionaires.

(2) Analyzes which were the wrong moves and which the right ones.

(3) Converts the good moves into actions *you* can take.

(4) Compiles a wealth-building program for each reader to follow.

Your own personal Compu-Analysis "printout" begins with the first chapter!

Scott Witt

Contents

10   Promote Your Way to Prosperity   165

11   Reap Extra Windfalls with Little Effort   185

12   How to Make Your Profits Snowball   203

1

The Million-Dollar Blueprint
That Guarantees Riches

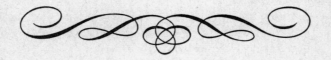

The first thing to realize about becoming a millionaire is that it's a lot more achievable than most people think. So achievable, in fact, that each year the number of millionares grows by 10,000. That means that one in every 1,075 Americans is now a millionaire.

How do they accomplish it? How can *you* do it? Read on.

THE MOST POWERFUL WEALTH-BUILDING STRATEGY

The methods of most self-made millionaires have been amazingly similar. One person may become rich in mail order, another in real estate, and a third in a service business—but nearly all use the same strategy to build their empires.

Some of today's self-made millionaires discovered the wealth-building strategy early and became rich quickly. Others, who took longer, found it only after continuous trial and error.

But if you were to do as I've done, and examine thousands of case histories of self-made millionaires, you'd make a surprising discovery. You'd discover that in nearly every case the same set of unwritten rules was responsible for their success.

You'd find that some self-made millionaires (let's call them SMMs) hit upon the rules by accident, others learned them through experience and diligent study, and still others were informed of them by relatives or business associates who had made the discovery earlier. But regardless of how they are learned, these rules comprise a Million-Dollar Blueprint That Guarantees Riches.

The same Blueprint that has made millions for others will work for you, except that you have an advantage. You won't have to wait for luck, prolonged struggle, or trial and error to reveal it to you. That's because the unwritten rules are now spelled out for the first time in the pages of this book.

The people who are already SMMs have done your homework for you. You'll find what they learned—and what they did—here in these pages, yours to apply from the start.

THE FIRST ELEMENT OF SUCCESS

There is one thing you must have before the Blueprint will work for you. It's not capital and it's not business genius—it's a burning desire for wealth.

The SMMs I'll be telling you about all started with such a burning desire, and it fired them into action. They didn't dream idly about winning a lottery or being remembered by a long lost uncle. They established their own goals and then set out to achieve them.

For example, an immigrant named Meshulam Riklis became an SMM after he grew tired of earning $110 per week at a desk job in Minneapolis. He set a goal for himself, and a big one it was: control of a multi-million dollar business empire. And he has achieved it.

He did it by using the assets of his very first company to buy control of another company, and then repeating the process as frequently as possible. (This is a technique you'll learn in Chapter 12.) His empire, known as Rapid-American, is involved with such things as manufacture of luggage and clothing, liquor distilling, chain store retailing, and textile production.

This conglomerate, worth hundreds of millions of dollars, began with a 29-year-old man whose chief asset was a burning desire. He converted that desire into a definite plan and then put that plan into action.

APPLY THE BLUEPRINT IN ANY FIELD

The Million-Dollar Blueprint works in any field. There are hundreds to choose from, including:

- Mail order
- Real estate
- Retailing
- Services

- Manufacturing
- Selling
- Fast foods
- Brokerage

- Training
- Show productions
- Advertising
- Publishing

The basic methods of rapid wealth-building are the same in these and all of the other million-dollar opportunities outlined in this book.

"How," you ask, "can real estate be likened to mail order? How can the same techniques used to make a killing in one field work in the other?"

Good question. The answer is that anybody can learn how to make a living in real estate or in mail order, but getting rich in either field (in *any* field) takes something extra. The "something extra" is what I call the Million-Dollar Blueprint.

Thus, I'm not going to teach you how to run a mail order business, a real estate business, or a service business. What I *am* going to do is demonstrate how you can teach yourself not only to run the business, but to become a millionaire doing it.

A COMPLETE SELF-ENRICHMENT PROGRAM

Here's what, together, we're going to do as you progress through the pages and chapters of this book:

(1) Pick the money-making field that is best for you.

(2) Make your enterprise the base of a million-dollar empire.

(3) Expand to the multi-million-dollar level you seek.

It's important to remember that all of the steps in the Million-Dollar Blueprint are documented by the case histories of today's most successful SMMs. These are no pie-in-the-sky theories. These are the very methods that have made these men and women rich, and these are the methods that spell the difference between eking out an income and becoming one of America's 200,000 + millionaires.

HOW TO CHART THE QUICKEST COURSE
TO FABULOUS WEALTH

From the day you make your very first business deal to the day you are satisfied with the size and scope of your empire, you will be following a *charted course*—a step-by-step program you have compiled yourself.

The advantages of having such a program are many:

- You have definite goals and proceed logically toward them.
- An ambitious project becomes easy, one step at a time.
- You know what your advance moves will be.
- You progress more rapidly because you are better organized.
- Planning and experience combine to build a richer future.

Arthur N. knew of the tremendous profits that can be made in buying and operating older apartment buildings, but never having been a landlord, the idea floored him.

"I was excited by the prospect but frightened by all the details involved," Arthur recalls, "until I put my program down on paper. Then I suddenly realized that all I had to do was *take one simple step at a time*. And I could see how easy it really was."

Here's the course Art charted for himself:

1. Buy four-unit building in the $20,000 range, paying about $5,000 down.
2. Improve the building and raise rents.
3. Sell the building for the higher value created by the steeper rents.
4. Use profits to buy a larger building.
5. Repeat the process of improving and selling, or, as an alternative, get the bank to increase the mortgage.
6. Use the proceeds to acquire more rental units.

Art now owns a total of 430 rental units in 23 buildings, giving him an annual rent roll of more than $1,000,000. His properties are worth more than $6,000,000, and his net worth exceeds

$1,500,000—all on an initial investment of $5,000!

It's easy to understand how Art might have been floored by the prospect of owning and managing six-million dollars worth of real estate. But running a four-unit building was entirely feasible. And as each of the steps was accomplished, the next step also became feasible.

THE BIGGER YOUR GOAL, THE BIGGER YOUR INCOME

While most SMMs work hard, they work no harder than thousands of other people who struggle along merely to bring home an average living. The difference is in their goals.

The goal of many people is merely to have a business of their own. Once they get it, they're satisfied. They are definitely not SMM material.

Meshulam Riklis, on the other hand, knew from the start that his first business was merely a stepping stone. It helped pave the way for his multi-million-dollar empire. That first enterprise was a printing equipment concern. Riklis *could* have spent all his time managing this one firm. Instead, he delegated much of the management to others while he searched for other firms to acquire.

Your own wealth-building program may not be similar to Riklis', but your basic concept should be the same. For example, your plan may be to operate a string of specialty restaurants. Certainly, learn thoroughly how to operate your first establishment. But once that's under your belt, delegate authority to others as you open new branches.

One of the most successful American money-makers of all time was Bernard Baruch. He put it better than I could when he said:

"The first requisite for making a lot of money is to want to make a lot of money."

A San Francisco man, George Mardikian, wanted to make so much money that his wife would be able to buy whatever her heart desired. He didn't have much money when he entered the restaurant business, but he had a big goal. And, as a symbol of that goal, he wrote his wife a post-dated check for $50,000. He told her that when the date arrived, she was to cash the check, buying whatever she happened to want at the time.

The date arrived and Mrs. Mardikian did cash the check. The

money was there because George Mardikian had set the big goal
for himself.

HOW TO MOBILIZE YOUR WEALTH-BUILDING POWERS

Right now, before I reveal the Million-Dollar Blueprint, I
want to let you in on one of the most important wealth-building
secrets you'll ever learn—in this book or anywhere. It can be stated
in just 12 words. But knowing those 12 words will make you a
wealth-builder instead of a mere income-earner.

Are you ready? Here it is:

Any successful business can become the basis of a million-dollar empire.

Please read it again. Yes, I'm telling you that *any* successful
business can become the basis of a million-dollar empire. What
does this mean to you? It means that if you build a successful
business, you can then boost it to the million-dollar level. I don't
mean a million dollars in sales, I mean more than that. I mean a
business that puts *you* in the million-dollar net worth category.

"O.K., Scott Witt," you say, "you've made the statement.
Now prove it."

You've already seen some of the proof. You saw how
Meshulam Riklis became a millionaire many times over starting
with a small printing equipment concern, and how Arthur N. made
a tiny four-unit apartment building the starting point of vast real
estate holdings. In future chapters, you'll watch the owner of a
small eatery become a magnate with nationwide restaurant and
hostelry holdings, and you'll see a lady start a simple little bakery
and then build it into a highly profitable corporation.

In all of these cases the same basic formula was followed.
Here's the formula:

Once you establish a success-pattern, repeat it over and over again.

The simplicity of this formula is equalled only by its power.
It's based on the fact that once you've learned how to be successful
by doing certain things, you have the confidence and ability to

repeat the process indefinitely.

"But," you say, "one business may not generate enough immediate cash to finance a new undertaking."

True, but the first success increases your power of *leverage*. Your proven track record opens up new sources of outside cash, whether it comes from borrowed funds, franchising, stock sales, mergers, or any of the other sophisticated techniques now open to you.

Thus, the way to mobilize your wealth-building powers, starting from scratch, is:

1. Build a small but successful business.
2. Use the leverage generated by that business to fire up new projects.
3. Keep repeating the process until you reach the dollar or scope level you established as your goal.

Naturally, there can be variations to this rule. Your business may be the kind that calls for *expansion* instead of repetition. (Instead of opening branches, you may choose to make your main location much larger.) But the same principles apply. Early success brings you the leverage power that you need to grow. Every major American corporation was built that way.

EXPAND NATIONWIDE

Many a small business has proven itself locally and then used that success to become a nationwide multi-million-dollar corporation. A good example is the one launched by Owen Murphy in an old barn behind his house in Adamsville, Pa.

Murphy held a patent to a vibrating chair designed to increase the blood circulation of the person using it. Convinced of its effectiveness because of his own medical training in the military service, Murphy set up a shop in the barn and then hired a man to sell his product door-to-door. The initial success led to the hiring of more than 300 other distributors coast-to-coast.

Owen Murphy's Niagara Therapy Corporation has made him a millionaire many times over, thanks to the cyclo-massage and heating units he developed and to the success-repetition process he employed.

HOW TO KEEP YOUR SELF-ENRICHMENT PROGRAM IN HIGH GEAR

Among the many traits shared by nearly all SMMs, and one which you should acquire, is *flexibility*. Times change, people change, conditions change—and this can require modification of your original operating plan.

Owen Murphy, for example, built his corporation on the basis of the good his products can do. Their effectiveness was proven by research laboratories. For years his emphasis rested almost solely on the benefits of using his products. But Americans were increasingly demanding good looks and fashion with whatever they bought.

Just as Henry Ford, years earlier, had to spruce up his "tin lizzies," Murphy finally conceded that his dealers were right in demanding better-appearing products.

When Murphy combined benefits with fashion, sales jumped. Flexibility paid off.

BE PREPARED FOR EXCITING NEW OPPORTUNITIES

Being flexible means you are ready when totally unexpected money-making opportunities present themselves to you. Your business can zoom in an entirely new—and much more profitable—direction.

Many people have opened office service bureaus, among them William Kelly, who hired two women to handle the typing, record-keeping, addressing, and other clerical chores assigned to his little company by other firms in the Detroit area.

Out of pending failure came an exciting new opportunity. An increasing amount of the work his company did was being taken over by automated machines that his customers were installing in their own offices. Thus the need for his services declined.

The opportunity? Providing trained people to run those machines. Kelly latched onto it, and thus was born the giant Kelly Services, providing temporary help to firms throughout the United States.

A small beginning in Detroit, flexibility that converted potential defeat into new success, and the success repetition factor on a coast-to-coast basis built Kelly's outfit into a major business empire.

THE POWER OF FLEXIBILITY
FOR MAKING A MILLION

Over coffee one day, I was explaining the success repetition factor to a group of business friends. Frankly, they were skeptical. (None was an SMM.) "You say *any* business can be brought up to the million-dollar level?" one of them asked. "Absolutely," I answered.

He smiled the way a poker player might when revealing a winning hand in a high-stakes game. "O.K., my friend," he said, "answer this one. My wife runs a little antique business from our home. It's profitable, so I presume you'd call it successful. But she could never repeat that success on a million-dollar scale. Antique shops are not the kind of thing you can make into a chain store or franchise operation, because anyone smart enough to run a shop for you is smart enough to run it for himself."

"True," I replied. "But the fact is that many million-dollar fortunes have been made in antiques, and from scratch, too." I then outlined the possibilities open to his wife. Among them:

- Becoming an antique wholesaler, selling only in quantity to retail dealers
- Operating antiques flea markets at many different locations
- Taking advantage of antique import opportunities
- Specializing in one high-priced line of antiques
- Scheduling antiques-oriented travel tours of the U.S. and foreign lands
- Conducting seminars on antique collecting and trading throughout the United States
- Purchasing entire estate contents and holding "mansion sales" (the rich man's version of the garage sale)

"A lot of people," I explained, "have become millionaires in the antique business. Your wife's success in a small business demonstrates her savvy about antiques. Now what she needs is to apply SMM techniques to what she already knows."

I've related this little conversation to show that million-dollar opportunities do indeed exist in every field, and any successful business can be the starting point. True, it takes imagination, it takes flexibility, and it takes proper application of the Million-Dollar Blueprint that will be introduced in this chapter, followed by the detailed plans to be unveiled in the chapters ahead. But it works. Thousands of SMMs are living proof of that.

YOU'RE READY FOR THE BLUEPRINT

You've already seen many of the attitudes and techniques that build the bank accounts of SMMs. Now I believe you are ready to see spelled out, move by move, the Million-Dollar Blueprint That Guarantees Riches.

Remember that these moves are the ones applied by the great majority of today's SMMs to build their empires. Although the Blueprint did not exist in written form until now, each of its moves has played a major role in creating today's new fortunes.

Together, let's see how *you* will be making the moves that will send new riches into your life.

MOVE ONE:
SET A SPECIFIC GOAL

SMMs visualize their empires long before the empires are created. They develop money minds that attract wealth ideas. As you'll see in Chapter 2, they think like, act like, and become millionaires.

If you already have an idea of the type of money-making field you'd like to enter, visualize the ultimate *scope* you want to reach. Such a goal might be the establishment of branches in every major American city, or a nationwide distribution network, or listing on a major stock exchange.

If you'd prefer to wait and examine the outstanding opportunities outlined later in this book, then set a *dollar* goal, and leave it at that for now. Three-million dollars' net worth in three years? Not at all out of the question. It's been done in less than one-third the time.

The importance of the goal is this: You now have something

definite to strive for, a focal point on which to aim your concentration and effort. As you'll see in the next chapter, visualization prepares your mind for the really BIG money-making ideas that await you.

MOVE TWO:
CHOOSE ONE OF TODAY'S
MILLION-DOLLAR OPPORTUNITIES

Opportunities for making big money have never been greater—but every SMM I've encountered picked a field that (1) can be "leveraged" in terms of cash and people, and (2) best matches his own talents, experience, and circumstances.

Using cash leverage and people leverage means that most of the money and most of the work in building an empire comes from outside sources. You'll learn how to do this in Chapters 3 and 9.

Chapters 4–6 tell how to choose the right million-dollar opportunity for *you*. This is important because, like everyone else in this world, you are a unique person. There are right businesses for you and wrong businesses for you. No one becomes an SMM until he's learned how to choose one of the "right" fields.

As you progress through this book, select several fields that interest you, and then, after you've completed the book and learned its principles, narrow the list to one.

MOVE THREE:
START SMALL AND LEARN YOUR FIELD INSIDE OUT

Every self-made millionaire is also a self-made expert. The way to become an expert in a given business is to run that business. You'll get to know every facet of the operation, and this will give you the know-how to deal with virtually any situation that develops.

Start your business with as little of your own cash as possible. In fact, you'll do this not only with your very first undertaking but with every subsequent business move you make. Financial leverage has been the basis of every sizable fortune.

Your initial business can be part time, and perhaps *should* be, so that you can be sustained by your existing source of income until your self-education process is well underway.

SMMs have found the first step is the most important step in the one-step-at-a-time approach. One move naturally propels them into the next. You'll learn *what* steps to take, and how to take them, in Chapter 7.

MOVE FOUR:
TEST EVERY MAJOR MOVE BEFORE YOU MAKE IT

Even the world's biggest and most successful corporations are constantly testing. They *know* the time and money that can be wasted by going into something—*anything*—cold. SMMs in particular know that almost any business idea or plan can be tested on a very small scale before it is put into regular operation.

So learn and practice the testing techniques explained in Chapter 8. And promise yourself that you'll never take an important step before testing it.

MOVE FIVE:
DUPLICATE OR EXPAND YOUR SUCCESSES

I gave you the formula earlier, and it's worth stating another time. Once you establish a success pattern, repeat it over and over again. Throughout the pages of this book you'll see one SMM after another do this, and enrich himself by doing it.

But to illustrate its logic, let me ask you these questions:

- Was Ray Kroc satisfied with just one McDonald's restaurant?
- Did J. Paul Getty search for no more oil wells after his first gusher came in?
- Did Cecil B. DeMille make one blockbuster movie and then call it quits?
- Did Frank Woolworth stop with his first successful variety store?
- Did Thomas Edison quit inventing after he created the Edison Universal Stock Printer?

The answer to all of these questions is, of course, no. Success-breeding-success is the key to building a good business into a great business. It's the key to your future empire. Pay particular heed to the repetition and expansion opportunities found in this book—the ones that apply to the field you select.

MOVE SIX:
INCREASE YOUR USE OF PEOPLE LEVERAGE

You may begin your money-making endeavors in a one-person enterprise to learn the ropes and spare the cash, but as you go, make increasing use of other people's talents and labor.

Few people, except perhaps rare artists, can achieve riches working alone. Everyone's time and everyone's talents have limitations. It was Andrew Carnegie, who rose from being a factory worker to become America's biggest steel magnate, who said: "The secret of success lies not in doing your own work, but in recognizing the right man to do it."

You'll discover how to pick other people who can make you rich when you read Chapter 9 in this book. People Leverage is one of the most effective tools at your command; use it.

MOVE SEVEN:
SPEED YOUR GROWTH
THROUGH GREATER CASH LEVERAGE

You'll recall my telling you earlier that each of your successes increases your power of cash leverage, that new sources of outside cash become available to you. Now's the time to really use that leverage in financing more projects or expanding your existing enterprise.

The procedure has a snowball effect:

The more you make, the more outside cash you attract. The more outside cash you attract, the bigger your operation. The bigger your operation, the more you make. The more you make . . .

Using the merger, franchising, and stock sale techniques outlined in Chapter 12, you can multiply your net worth *overnight*. Take stock sales as an example. The stock market almost never values a company at its real net worth. It rates the company on *potential*. Thus, one day you may own 100% of a company worth, say, a million dollars. Then you put one-third of its shares on the market, which recognizes great potential in your firm. The stocks comprising the one-third interest sell for one and one-half million dollars. Since you own *two*-thirds interest, your net worth has zoomed to three-million dollars. It's happened many times.

Mergers and franchising offer equally great opportunities, and you're going to learn how to make full use of them.

The Blueprint Will Work For You

Some of the techniques I've listed, particularly the later ones, may seem complex to you at this stage. But please remember the one-step-at-a-time approach. The accomplishment of each step makes the next one that much easier.

By the time you reach the later steps, you'll be ready for them. You'll also be able to afford to hire the specialists who can arrange stock, franchise, and merger deals for you.

The one-step-at-a-time approach makes earning a million dollars a lot easier, doesn't it? O.K., let's take the first step. It's detailed in the next chapter.

2

How to Think Like, Act Like, and Become a Millionaire

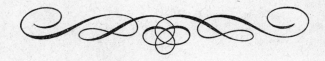

Born to be rich. How many times have you heard that said about somebody who has achieved one financial success after another? Nearly everything such a person does turns into a pot of gold, and the awe-struck spectators think it's all because of some "magic" born within him.

Self-made millionaires are the first to point out that their wealth-building abilities were *acquired*, not inherited. And it's been demonstrated over and over again that it's never too late to acquire these abilities.

In fact, age is hardly a factor in determining wealth-success. Consider these case histories:

- Harland Sanders was 66 when a new highway took traffic away from his restaurant and he began peddling his Kentucky Fried Chicken recipe nationwide. At an age when most people are retired, he became a millionaire.

- Ray Kroc, the founder of the McDonald's chain, worked at many jobs until he discovered the success formula that made him a millionaire well past the age of 40.

- Rick Byers sells real estate and along the way has become so successful at it that he's acquired more than $5,000,000 worth of property for himself. He's 28.
- Carl Magee was 70 when he conceived of the idea of a coin-operated parking meter as a means of assuring that downtown parking spaces would not be hogged by store employees, leaving few spaces for shoppers. His firm became the principal maker of the meters in the United States.
- William Lear, whose empire was built in aviation and electronics, made his first million before reaching the age of 30.

So you can see that age is not important in becoming an SMM. You can do it at any time. But you can't merely sit back and wait for it to happen. To become a millionaire, you have to think like one and act like one.

DEVELOP A MONEY MIND AND REAP GIANT REWARDS

Now don't get me wrong. When I advise you to think like and act like a millionaire, I don't mean you should, with limited funds, start "living it up." I don't mean jetting off to Acapulco every other weekend or buying a Rolls Royce for trips to the supermarket, at least not yet.

What I do mean is that you should start developing the same kind of *money mind* that has opened up vast wealth-building opportunities for today's self-made rich.

You can start developing your money mind today, this very instant, by learning how to:

- Spot opportunity in everyday occurrences
- Adapt current trends to new circumstances
- Eagerly use other people's money
- Find important needs and fill them
- Expand your success cycle

These are the five key ingredients of a money mind. Let's take a closer look at them.

SPOT OPPORTUNITY IN EVERYDAY OCCURRENCES

"The difference between a self-made millionaire and the ne'er-do-well," a wise and rich man once told me, "is that the millionaire has developed the ability to see *profit* situations where the average person would merely see *problem* situations."

Opportunities for tremendous profit appear before us every day, and by training our minds to look for them, they're ours to benefit from.

A truck driver in Tampa, Florida, spotted opportunity when he dealt with the problem of obtaining a home for his wife and himself. Jim Walter saw an ad in a local newspaper for a so-called "shell house," a structure the builder would erect on the customer's lot. The exterior would be finished, with the interior left to the buyer to complete.

Mr. Walter became so fascinated with the concept as a means of providing low-cost housing for those who could not afford to buy completed homes that he convinced the builder to go into partnership with him, promoting and selling the homes on a larger scale than the builder had been doing.

Jim Walter became a multi-millionaire, and his Jim Walter Corporation became the second largest home sales corporation in the United States. And it was all because Mr. Walter spotted opportunity when another person might have merely seen a cheap way to acquire a new home for his own family.

Joseph Katz, who has become one of America's most successful producers of printed gift wrappings, started his fortune-building process when his home city of Pittsburgh faced a major problem—a flood that inundated the business area.

Inspecting the area, Mr. Katz noticed that, despite the chaos and turmoil, a lot of people were out with their cameras, taking pictures. Knowing that these pictures would be valuable, he bought up the exposed film of every person who would sell it to him.

He took those pictures to another city (electricity having been cut off in Pittsburgh), developed the film, and saw that the prints could be the basis of an "instant" news magazine. He convinced a printer in Cleveland to print the magazine on credit, published 100,000 copies, and shipped them back to Pittsburgh. He beat the local newspapers by four days, and quickly sold out all his copies.

How You Can Do It

The Jim Walters and Joseph Katzes of the future are the people who today are constantly on the lookout for profitable situations. As you've seen, these situations are not hidden. All it takes is looking at things with a new perspective—a *money* perspective.

Here's how to spot opportunity in everyday occurrences:

1. Be money-conscious 24 hours a day. Every time you see a problem or unusual situation, ask yourself, "What could I do, as a businessman, to solve the problem or deal with the situation?"

2. Carry a notebook with you wherever you go. Use it to jot down your "money-project" ideas. Fleeting thoughts which might soon be forgotten can become some of your biggest potential moneymakers.

3. At the end of each week, review the notes you've made. And after several weeks, you'll be amazed at how you have honed your profit-spotting powers. You'll have amassed a collection of wealth-building ideas, a good many of them in related fields.

4. Going over the related items, you'll come up with additional profit possibilities that you hadn't thought of until now.

One man who has made excellent use of this system is Al T., who is well on his way to becoming an SMM (he's worth $350,000, less than a year after launching his wealth-building program).

Speaking of his "money-project notebook," Al says: "It's amazing, but it works. When several notations in my pad are on similar subjects, they fuel my mind with still more ideas on the same subject. That's how I started my first mail order business."

Al sells printed forms to business firms, specializing in debt collection letters. He'd noted that many companies assign their debts to collection agencies, thus giving up 50% or more of the amount collected. And often, all the collection companies do to get the money is send out letters. Enabling creditors to do this for themselves has saved them a lot of money—and made a lot for Al.

ADAPT CURRENT TRENDS
TO NEW CIRCUMSTANCES

Some of the best new opportunities can be merely adaptations of older money-making methods. Joseph Katz progressed from one business deal to another in the printing field until he hit upon the idea of selling attractive wrappings for holiday gifts.

But other firms were selling the same type of product, and his problem was finding himself a wedge to get through the door. That wedge was a developing trend: self-service. People were loading their own shopping baskets in supermarkets and picking out their own items in discount stores. So he got the idea of putting gift paper on rolls instead of in the usual flat sheets, and placing the rolls on racks for shoppers to choose from.

That was adaptation number one. But sales didn't really reach their stride until he thought up adaptation number two. In the same stores offering his gift-paper rolls, Mr. Katz noted that candy-makers were selling *multiple packages* of candy bars. Why not adapt this for his own use? He did—offering three-pack rolls— and profits skyrocketed. His Papercraft Corporation has become the biggest producer of gift wrappings in the world.

How You Can Do It

What works in one field, as Joseph Katz discovered, often works equally well in another. Use your money-project notebook to jot down unique business methods that intrigue you, whether or not they're in a field you are considering. Reviewing these later will often give you ideas on how they can be adapted to the business you've decided upon. Some examples:

- A New York State man noticed that teenagers were washing cars in the driveways of their customers. He figured the same convenience factor could work with auto tune-ups. So he launched a thriving business by offering to do tune-ups and oil changes in car owners' driveways—sparing them the bother of dropping the car off at a garage.

- A Californian, whose hobby was electronics, noticed the increasing use, by large supermarkets and department stores, of computerized cash registers that also keep records of inventory. Knowing of the rapidly declining cost of micro-processing units, he developed a relatively inexpensive unit that would allow small independent businessmen to computerize their operations just the way big businesses have done.

- An Ohioan who ran a picture-framing shop noticed that national firms such as Readers Digest and Time-Life sell related products, including books and records. So why couldn't he do the same thing, selling products related to his own business? He put a mini art gallery in a vacant store next to his existing shop, knowing that many of his customers were already interested in art. He since has opened several other combined framing-and-art outlets.

EAGERLY USE OTHER PEOPLE'S MONEY

Part of Jim Walter's success in selling shell houses came with the financing he offered to buyers. But, of course, he soon found that there was a limit to the financing he could offer by himself. Over the years he has made increasing use of outside mortgage money to offer purchasers of his homes. And to enable his corporation to grow even more rapidly, he has sold equity in the form of stocks and bonds, just as I recommended you should do in the previous chapter.

Many people have been brought up on the old adage, "Better go to bed supperless than rise in debt." That may be true, to an extent, in personal finances, but it is totally *un*true in business.

The leverage provided by other people's money is the leverage that will build your fortune. You'll recall that Joseph Katz obtained his first important success—the special Pittsburgh flood magazine—by convincing the printer to do the work on credit. At another time, before he had made his first million, Mr. Katz saw a bargain in coated paper close-outs. He offered the manufacturer an attractive price. Not having the money to pay for the merchandise, he asked for and got credit of 90 days. The goods were sold, and the debt repaid, ahead of schedule.

Naturally, credit must be used wisely. You must be convinced of the potential of your business plan before using OPM. But once you do have a good plan, OPM can do a lot more for you than if you

FIND IMPORTANT NEEDS AND FILL THEM

The person with a money mind is constantly looking for needs that he might be able to fill. William Lear—mentioned earlier in this chapter—has made a lifelong habit of that. He began as a schoolboy, at a time when cars frequently stalled on the road. Often the trouble was a breakdown of carbons in the distributor. He made a practice of carrying carbon in his pocket, and he earned good spending money supplying stalled motorists with the very thing that was needed.

Later, after becoming a radio engineer, he came up with the idea of installing radios in automobiles. Thus was born the brand name Motorola. After that, he noticed that while Air Force bombers could use autopilots, the units were too bulky for fighter planes. So he developed a unit that would fit nicely into the smaller aircraft.

Then came the now-famous Learjets—which so many of today's SMMs use to travel between various parts of their business empires. Jets had worked well for commercial aviation, why not for private and business use? Bill Lear found another need and filled it.

It was the same with stereo tape decks in automobiles—another Bill Lear innovation. He had found an entertainment need and filled it.

How You Can Do It

I go into greater detail on finding and filling needs in Chapter 7, but for now I'd like to pass along this advice:

Every time you see a need, jot it down in your money-project notebook.

Do this even if you can't conceive of a way that you could personally fill that need. Your collection of unfilled needs will grow, and as other facets of your money mind grow, you may uncover theretofore undreamed-of ways of filling those needs.

Mail order entrepreneur Al T.—the man who's been so successful selling business forms—was not and is not a writer. "I have trouble even composing a letter home to my wife," he sheepishly admits.

But one of his notebook entries concerned debt collection letters, and every time he came across it, it intrigued him. Finally convinced that the idea was a good one, he hired a freelance writer to compose some debt collection letters for him. The writer also prepared his sales literature.

The freelancer who had the ability to carry out Al's idea is now one of his top employees, earning more than $20,000 per year. But Al—the man with the idea—is taking home more than double that amount. And, as I reported earlier, he's one-third of the way toward becoming an SMM, thanks to the equity he's built up in his business.

EXPAND YOUR SUCCESS CYCLE

The story of Kemmons Wilson is the story of a person who has had one success lead directly to another. His first was when he had a popcorn concession in a Kansas movie theater. Using the working capital left over from that, he bought some second-hand pinball machines and placed them in restaurants and pharmacies. The pinball enterprise gave him money with which to build a home for himself. Then he borrowed on the home to enlarge his pinball and vending machine route.

When, a year later, he sold the house for more than twice what it had cost him, he recognized the profits to be made in real estate. So he began building homes, buying existing apartment buildings with little cash down, and obtaining commerical structures as well.

One day, in the early 1950's, Kemmons Wilson took his family on a jaunt to Washington, D.C. They were extremely disappointed with the motels they encountered en route. This convinced him to enter the motel business—building four such hostelries in the Memphis area. Thus was born his giant Holiday Inn empire.

The lesson to be learned here is the same one conveyed in a slightly different manner in the previous chapter of this book—the fact that success breeds success.

And Kemmons Wilson has not stopped with motels—as giant as his corporation now is. Not only has the Holiday Inn brandname been imprinted on numerous consumer products, his holdings include subsidiaries and other businesses in the fields of transportation, health care, home furnishings, manufacturing, computer technology, and, of course, construction. Total value? Well over a billion dollars.

For Kemmons Wilson, it's been a long and fruitful journey from that first $50 popcorn machine. It's also been a continuous expansion of his success cycle.

While your own first success can lead naturally to other successes you don't presently envision, you should begin preparing for them now. Even as you begin your first venture, insert ideas and plans for future expansion and diversification in your money-project notebook.

RID YOURSELF OF FABLES, FEARS, AND FAILURES

It's been known for thousands of years, but some people even today fail to recognize it. Some two thousand years ago, the Roman poet Virgil said, "They can conquer who believe they can." Two hundred years ago, the British lexicographer and author, Samuel Johnson, put it another way: "Self-confidence is the first requisite to great undertakings." And today, almost any SMM will tell you that *knowing that success would have to come* played an important role in the fortune-building process.

True, nearly all SMMs have faced occasional discouragement. But it takes just one important victory to wipe out early failures. Sports figures have demonstrated this time and again. When a young boxer named Gene Tunney fought Harry Greb, Tunney was mauled. The first punch broke his nose. This was followed by slashes over both eyes, cut lips, and a bloodied face. Tunney lost that fight, but moments after it was over he demanded a return bout. There were *four* return bouts, and Tunney won every time. In fact, he never again lost a fight to anyone.

Among his many baseball achievements, Ty Cobb is perhaps best remembered for his record-breaking number of stolen bases achieved in 1915. In that same year, at least ten other players had better performance records, percentage-wise. And Cobb himself had his share of failures that year. But as Gene Tunney was to do later, he came back for more, and the "more" was victory.

Cobb, incidentally, was just as shrewd a businessman as he

was a baseball player. Unlike so many of his colleagues, he was able to parlay his baseball earnings into a lifelong fortune.

A luminary in another field of endeavor, movie producer Mike Todd, had this to say: "I've never been poor, only broke. Being poor is a frame of mind. Being broke is a temporary situation." In line with this, let's see how SMMs convert failure to success by ridding themselves of fables and fears.

FABLE-FEAR NO. 1: I WON'T SUCCEED

There might be ten times as many millionaires walking the streets today if it weren't for the fact that most people with good money-making ideas never try them out. They literally kill their brainstorms with worry about failure, and they give in too easily to discouragement from well-meaning friends and relatives.

Susan F. almost became one of these statistics. Everyone told her that her plan for a campground for travel trailers and motor homes wouldn't work. A young widow with small children to support, she had somehow managed to hold on to the rural acreage her husband had bought for possible future use as a summer retreat.

"Only because Charlie had bought it for a song with very low mortgage payments was I able to keep it," Susan recalls. "Before he died, Charlie and I had occasionally rented camper-type vehicles, so I was aware of the booming campground industry. And I *knew* my property, not far from an interstate highway, was a perfect setup for such a campground."

Friends tried to convince her that her lack of business experience, her obligations to her children, and the odds against success would defeat her. But Susan wouldn't give in. She increased the mortgage on her home, traded in the family station wagon for an older car, and took out a bank loan to pay for the relatively minor improvements the property needed.

The next year her campground was listed in several of the national directories that recreational vehicle owners use as vacation guides, and her endeavor was an instant success. She now owns two other campgrounds as well as a recreational vehicle dealership.

The key to Susan's success? She *knew* her plan was a good one. Her friends didn't know it, her relatives didn't know it, but *she* did and, therefore, she acted.

FABLE-FEAR NO. 2: I FAILED ONCE,
I'LL FAIL AGAIN

No one—that's right—*no one* succeeds every time, but please remember Gene Tunney, Ty Cobb, and Mike Todd. All of them had their share of early failures, and so have most SMMs you'll encounter in this book or elsewhere.

Why don't failures set such people back? Because of two rules that you should learn well:

1. SMMs make failure a prelude to success. They realize that every good plan must go through a testing period. Each preliminary failure brings new knowledge and improvement.
2. The law of averages is in your favor. Five small losses are easily canceled by one big gain. It was printer, publisher, and craftsman Elbert Hubbard who said, "A failure is a man who has blundered but is not able to cash in on the experience."

Two examples illustrate these rules. A man who decided to start a publishing firm almost lost everything with his first book. Hardly had the business-related publication hit the streets before some of the information it contained suddenly became outdated. From this experience, he hit upon the idea of publishing business information in *looseleaf form*—so the data could be continually updated. It was an innovation in the publishing field, his company became a giant among American publishers, and his brainchild has since been adopted by many imitators. This man's failure was a prelude to success.

And Earl Prevette, a man who reached the pinnacle of success as a salesman, tells how the law of averages worked for him. In his book, *How to Turn Your Ability Into Cash* (Prentice-Hall, Inc.), Prevette tells of the time he made 1800 calls over the telephone without getting a bite. He was promoting a life insurance sales plan, and he knew the law of averages couldn't let him down.

He was right, because shortly thereafter sales began to pour in. The upshot is that in less than a month he netted $3600, and a subsequent bonus doubled that figure. It was just one of many occasions when the law of averages proved itself to Earl Prevette.

FABLE-FEAR NO. 3: IT'S A GOOD PLAN, BUT I COULD NEVER DO IT

Nonsense. If you *want* to do it, you can. Remember the one-step-at-a-time approach mentioned in the previous chapter? It's a great confidence-builder, and I've seen it work many times. You'll recall that Arthur N. parlayed $5,000 into a personal fortune of $1,500,000 by taking one simple step at a time.

Here are some other examples:

- A radio engineer was awed at the prospect of starting a local radio station of his own. But, convinced the area needed it, he proceeded one step at a time, obtaining an excellent spot on the dial, setting up his station in a trailer, erecting a tower, and going on the air. It quickly knocked out the competition and won many awards. It's now in a modern studio building.

- A news reporter watched the success of fast-food establishments with envy. Having been trained to cover stories step-by-step, he drew up plans for his own fast-food establishment in the same manner. He developed a method of using precooked meats for sandwiches. His first store was a success and he's now working on the franchising step of his long range plan.

- The husband of a travel agent spotted an opportunity for providing businessmen with international travel services meeting their individual and, often, last-minute needs. It was a giant project requiring a system of overseas communications, strong financial backing, and careful coordination. But he charted a course, took it step by step, and now is providing a valuable and lucrative service for some of the nation's largest corporations.

Can you name the one factor that enabled all of the people you've been reading about to rid themselves of their fears and fables and overcome any early failures? In a word, it was *visualization*.

MAKE VISUALIZATION YOUR SILENT PARTNER

Many budding entrepreneurs start out with active partners. They do this to bring in financing, specialized knowledge, or just plain labor. But once their enterprises begin to flourish, most of these people buy out their partners. A real entrepreneur can't share control with another person any longer than he has to. And he shouldn't. The old adage about too many cooks spoiling the broth is more true in business than in any other field. Yet, one "partnership" that remains a lifelong affair with most self-made millionaires is visualization.

Put simply, visualization is mentally picturing your enterprise as you wish it to be. Not just daydreaming, but laying out before your mind's eye the exact nature of the business, what it will do, how it will be run, whom it will deal with, the kind of money it will bring in.

Here are just some of the advantages of visualization:

- You have a definite goal to work toward.
- You think and move positively.
- You build confidence in yourself, and the confidence of others in you.
- You know your business inside out and are prepared for each progressive step as the time for it approaches.
- You have the stick-to-it-iveness needed to become a millioniare because you know it can and will happen.

SMMs everywhere attest to the almost magical powers of visualization. They go by the credo that nothing that is not first envisioned can be accomplished. How many times, in reading or hearing an outstanding success story, have you detected this theme: "He (or she) saw what others didn't see."

Naturally that person saw what others didn't see! That's because the person had visualization—and that's why he or she is a millionaire and the others are not.

Nobody saw much of a future for Joseph Hrudka. He might have been considered a typical American boy, with a passion for cars. He tinkered with them, he raced them. In fact, his passion for four-wheeled vehicles caused him to drop out of college so he could devote more time to them.

He knew that someday his fortune would be built on cars. Others, not sharing his visualization, predicted he'd wind up as a grease-monkey in some two-bit repair shop.

Of course, they had some reason to believe this because Joe did spend a lot of his time in automotive shops—particularly the speed shops. But what he knew and others didn't was that he was searching for an automobile-connected business idea. And he found it. A problem Joe and his racing friends often encountered involved exhaust gaskets, which frequently blew out at high racing temperatures.

He envisioned adapting the type of gasket used in high-temperature diesel and aircraft engines for use in racing cars and other souped-up vehicles. These special gaskets were made of asbestos.

So Joe got some asbestos and started making gaskets in the garage of his home. The same heat resistance that was proven in commercial engines was effective in the kind of vehicles Joe was dealing with.

He had a friend sell his new product at the friend's speed shop, and they sold like the proverbial hotcakes. Other retail outlets demanded them, and before long Joe was forced by business volume to move out of his garage and into a series of successively larger manufacturing plants.

Within four years, his company, known as Mr. Gasket, had made Joe Hrudka a millionaire. And a few years later, in the early 1970's, he sold his company to a giant corporation, pocketing more than $11-million. His visualization had made him a multi-millionaire.

VISUALIZATION CARRIES YOU THROUGH

Visualization is effective in launching your million-dollar career, but it becomes even more so as you progress. That's because after you've seen its powers really work for you, you put it to greater use.

A Minnesotan named Jeno Paulucci borrowed $2500 to go into the food business with a partner. He had found that most Chinese foods were bland tasting, and he envisioned that, with some good Italian spices such as his mother had always used, these foods could be made a lot more palatable.

After founding the Chun King Company, he visualized making sales to large supermarkets. He knew that someday his firm would be a big name in the food business, and this self-inspired confidence carried over in his conversations with food executives. Who knows? It may be that they thought his company was *already* a giant corporation. In any event, he did nothing to discourage the impression. He didn't tell them his products were canned in a Quonset hut and that his office was a tiny box-like affair paneled with factory-second wallboards.

If they thought he had a raft of secretaries, worked in front of solid oak paneling, and directed a corporation with far-flung holdings, it was only because Jeno Paulucci knew that this was the way things were to become. And, naturally, they did. Mr. Paulucci was able to buy out his partner. Sales skyrocketed. Profits zoomed. Having achieved his goal—or at least that part of his goal—he sold his business for $63-million—cash.

But visualization continued to work for Jeno Paulucci. Having proven that he could sell *Chinese* food with Italian flavorings, he knew he could do just as well selling *Italian* food with those same flavorings. Thus was born his firm, Jeno's Inc., which sells frozen pizzas and other foods. Those sales amount to more than $100 million per year.

START VISUALIZING TODAY

The wonderful power of visualization can be yours, beginning right now. In fact, by following the advice already given in this chapter, you've already started to use it. Entries made in your money-project notebook have launched your "silent partnership" with visualization.

Now make some more entries. The initial ones, of course, dealt with business ideas. This time, write down the kind of fortune you'd like to control. Don't be bashful about it, make it big. And, as you progress through this book and zero in on the specific means of building your fortune, make entries explaining what your enterprise is to become.

Let's say that you decide to own and operate a theme park, one of those multi-million-dollar extravaganzas that have sprouted up all over the country as offshoots of what Walt Disney started in Anaheim years ago.

Here's what your entry might say:

I will acquire land for, build, and operate a major theme park. It will be at least 100 acres in size, and will attract hundreds of thousands of visitors each year.

Admittedly, this is an ambitious undertaking. Heretofore, most theme parks have been developed by large corporations. But didn't Joseph Katz, Joseph Hrudka, and Jeno Paulucci break into fields then dominated by the giants? And didn't these men become giants themselves?

Once you've made your entry, take it to heart. Think about it, dream about it, scheme about it, plan for it in every available moment. Soon you'll come up with ideas on how your plans can be tested on a small scale, perfected, and then enlarged via the success-breeding-success cycle.

In the theme park example, part of your visualization process would soon have you visiting as many existing parks as you can. You would note that theme parks are indeed built around a theme. (The "Magic Kingdom" of Walt Disney, the safari theme of Florida's Busch Gardens, the "chocolate world" of Hersheypark.) And your reading on the subject would inform you that many parks began in a very small fashion:

- Busch Gardens was originally just that; a walk-through flower garden.
- Knott's Berry Farm in California was launched with small entertainment features to keep diners occupied while they waited for seats at the Knott family restaurant.
- Hersheypark in Pennsylvania began as a typical community park with benches and a bandshell.

Thus, your visualization would tell you that it is possible to start a family entertainment facility on a small scale, continually enlarging the facility around the original theme and adopting new themes.

And your one-step-at-a-time approach would have you putting

a down payment on rural acreage near a major interstate highway, installing a small entertainment facility or museum-like attraction on one part of the property, using the initial success to build your leverage, employing the leverage to expand the park and attract more people, and ultimately meeting the goal set out in your money-project notebook. *Your* visualization may not involve a theme park, but the method is the same. Start putting it to work for you right now.

ATTRACT WEALTH IDEAS LIKE A MAGNET

After I had pointed out the power of visualization to a friend one day, she commented, "I can see its effectiveness, but first you must have something *to* visualize! Sure, I'd like to make a lot of money, but I have trouble thinking up ideas."

I hope she reads this book and particularly this chapter. In fact, I'm going to give her a copy. Then she'll know that just as a magnet *naturally* attracts metals, any person can *naturally* attract wealth ideas.

What do I mean by *naturally?* I mean that just as a magnet attracts items without any apparent effort, a person can find and attract wealth ideas which—whether he knows it or not—are all around him all the time. Once you've tuned up your money mind, it's a natural, almost effortless, process.

Consider these experiences:

- B.F. Hamilton used a kitchen match to light his cigar, and then didn't know where to deposit the match without danger of fire. This gave him the idea for a kitchen match container, one compartment containing fresh matches, the other one being a repository for spent matches. He quickly sold housewares stores on the idea, and following the success-breeding-success formula, his Hamilton Cosco, Inc. went on to produce literally thousands of different household items.

- A Michigan housewife needed a stronger household cleanser. The items on the market just weren't good enough for her. So she did a little research and came up with ingredients for a more effective product. Perhaps you've heard of it. It's called Spic and Span.

• A man visiting Cisco, Texas, noticed a lot of activity at the town's little hotel. This young man had always wanted to be a banker, planning on that as his career. But detecting that boom-town hotels did exceptionally well, he bought the little one in Cisco with a $5,000 stake and some credit, and promptly forgot about about banking. His name; Conrad Hilton.

• Leo Gerstenzang wasn't even searching for a career when he found his big-money-maker. Merely wanting to help his wife bathe their baby, he devised a cotton swab to clean the ears, nose, and eyes. The product is now used for a multitude of hygiene chores. It's known as Q-Tips.

• A Baltimore druggist named George Bunting noticed that the skin salves then available had unpleasant odors and that they stained clothing. Customers complained about this, and so he put some soothing ingredients into a cosmetic cream. The first customer to try it raved about it, saying it "knocks eczema out." The statement led Bunting to name the product Noxzema. The rest, as they say, is history.

HOLD ON TO YOUR WEALTH IDEAS

The truth is, we *all* get money-making ideas similar to those just listed. And the trouble is, most people soon forget these ideas. The pressure of everyday living, family problems, other interests and the like cause our minds to soon change course, and a potential money-maker is lost forever.

This is where, once again, your money-project notebook is an invaluable ally. Carry it with you wherever you go, and be sure to jot down such ideas as they occur to you. Keep it at hand no matter where you are—sleeping, eating, working, visiting with friends. That's what inventor Walter Jinotti does. He's developed a lot of medical equipment that is sold across the United States; equipment which has helped thousands of patients. And many of his inventions stemmed from ideas that hit him like a flash. Fortunately, he jotted them down.

You'll find that successful people in all walks of life do this. U.S. Steel's Roger Blough, one of America's executive giants, told an interviewer about it a few years ago. Mr. Blough pointed out that it not only helps you remember ideas that come to you, but it clears your mind so you can go on to something else related to your business plans. If that "something else" is getting started with little or none of your own cash, you can relieve your mind by reading the next chapter.

3

Use Little or None of Your Own Cash

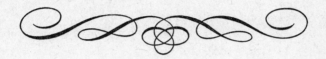

Is it really possible to become a self-made millionaire starting with no cash? Ask some of today's SMMs and you'll find out. A great many of them started that way. As this chapter shows, you can, too.

You're going to learn the No-Cash Empire-Building Formula, a plan that enables any ambitious person to start with zero cash (except for a few incidental supplies) and climb rapidly up the financial ladder.

Naturally, if you have a bit of cash to invest, your start can be bigger. But that's the wonderful thing about the formula. You can enter it at any point. You can start at the bottom rung with no cash, even with no way of getting cash advances. Or, depending on what resources and credit rating you have, you can join the program at a higher level—that much closer to the top.

As soon as possible, you'll be using other people's money, and you'll continue to use it throughout your financial career. No matter how little or how much capital of your own you have available, the greatest part of your investment should and will come from outside sources such as those listed in this chapter.

DON'T LET LACK OF MONEY HOLD YOU BACK

Leverage, as you know, means using a little of your own money to control a lot of somebody else's money. You use leverage every time you buy something on time, whether it's a car, a home, or an appliance. Your down payment gives you full use of the item purchased, even though the bulk of the money was put up by the bank, seller, or finance company.

There's an important difference when you use leverage in business. When you buy a product for your personal use, *you* have to make the monthly payments. When you borrow money for business purposes, your *customers* make the monthly payments.

That's what enabled Arthur N. (mentioned in the first chapter) to start with $5,000 of his own cash and rapidly gain control of $1,500,000 worth of real estate. Each time he made a down payment on an apartment house, that was the last payment he made out of his own cash. The monthly mortgage payments came out of his rent receipts. And each subsequent purchase of a new apartment building came either from (1) profits from the sale of an earlier building, or (2) refinancing of an earlier building made possible by its increased value.

Thus, Art multiplied his original investment 300 times. ($5,000 × 300 = $1,500,000.) That's what we call leverage, and it can be used in many fields other than real estate.

"But," you say, "I haven't *got* $5,000 to start with." Never mind. You can start with nothing. Well, nothing other than perhaps the cost of some incidental supplies such as paper, a little gasoline for your car, some postage stamps, etc.

MAKE A MILLION STARTING FROM ZERO

Of all the self-made millionaires I've encountered, I'd say at least half began without putting up any cash of their own to get started. These SMMs knew the value of OPM right from the start. The fact is, you have, *right now*, just about all you need to get started building your multi-million-dollar empire. Look at this list of resources, and I'll bet you have most of them:

- Time available for your money project
- A lifetime of experience
- Working space (a desk, a corner, a room, a basement, a garage, etc.)
- Family members able to conduct some of the chores
- Loan eligibility (you have more than you think)
- Visualization

Learning how one person used these resources to build a personal fortune will illustrate how you can do the same thing. In fact, you are probably far better off than Phil D. was when he started.

Phil was severely injured in a horseback riding accident. His long hospitalization cost him his job, his life savings, and his home. Shortly after his release from the hospital he had to move with his wife and three children into an apartment paid for out of welfare funds.

Here's how Phil made use of his remaining resources:

Time: Having plenty of that, he used it at first to read library books on business. One such book gave him an idea for a newsletter on public relations.

Experience: His job, before he lost it, had been for a public relations agency. He had many contacts in the PR industry, and his idea was to prepare a monthly newsletter for small business firms that could benefit from free publicity.

Working Space: Phil set aside a spare bedroom as his newsletter office. For $12 he bought an extension telephone and wired it into that room, and his eldest son moved in a desk, the family typewriter, and a file cabinet.

Family Members: His wife and all of the children happily chipped in on the project—not financially (because they couldn't) but with labor. In the beginning, before he was fully recovered, they ran errands for Phil, and later, after publication had started, they helped stuff envelopes.

Loan Eligibility: As you might expect, a family on welfare is just about a zero loan prospect. Thus, Phil didn't even try for loans from the usual sources. But he had wisely chosen a business in which the *customers* provide loans. His newsletters sold for $36 per year, cash in advance. Subscribers, in effect, were lending Phil $36 before even receiving the first issue of their subscriptions. He sold enough subscriptions to his business contacts to pay for the mailing of sales letters to other likely prospects.

Visualization: Phil knew that there was tremendous potential in the newsletter industry, and he visualized earning much more than was promised by the book. He knew that the Success Repetition Factor could make him a rich man.

The outcome is that Phil's newsletter was instantly profitable, and within a year he was earning $18,000 from it. On the basis of this success, he launched five other newsletters within a period of three years. His business (now located in its own freestanding office building) is conservatively estimated to be worth more than a million dollars.

HOW A GIANT CORPORATION BEGAN FROM SCRATCH

Ross Siragusa also got part of his starting stake from his customers. That came after he borrowed $3,400 on his car and furniture to start manufacturing small radios in the corner of a garage. After the manufacturing setup was functioning smoothly, he used his last $200 to take a bus ride to Pittsburgh, where he was able to convince the head of a large chain store company to buy 250 radios. He also got the man to promise to pay for the radios promptly after receiving the bill for them. (Common practice is to wait several months.)

Siragusa was able to use the money received from the retailer to pay off his own suppliers. This got him started, and one success led to another. His company branched out into radio-phonographs, television sets, and home appliances. I'm sure you've heard of the Admiral Corporation.

THE NO-CASH EMPIRE-BUILDING FORMULA

Whether or not you have possessions such as a car or a home to borrow money on, you can get started immediately in building your own financial empire. What you lack in cash or borrowing capacity you can make up by using the powerful techniques you're about to learn. Then, when your business is established and successful, conventional money sources will be fully available to you.

I'll give you the formula in outline form first and then explain it in more detail. Remember, you enter the program at whatever point is best for you under your present circumstances.

1. Start with no capital and no loan eligibility.
2. Use OPM, but no personal cash, to build your business.
3. Employ the "scale technique" to get started with minimum personal or OPM financing.
4. Speed your growth through initial profit plow-back.
5. Use the Success Repetition Factor for continued growth and expansion.

BOTTOM RUNG:
START WITH NO CAPITAL AND NO LOAN ELIGIBILITY

No money and no credit rating? A sizable proportion of today's self-made millionaires got started under the same circumstances. Here's how they did it:

1. Use of time and talent instead of money
2. Customer financing
3. Financing from partners or stockholders
4. Bankroll-building through OJT

Use one or combine several of these techniques to build a solid foundation for your million-dollar empire. Then you can climb rapidly up the succeeding rungs in the program. Let's see how you can do it.

Use Time and Talent to Build Your Fortune

There are literally hundreds of businesses that can be started with time and talent alone. Oh, a few dollars for incidental supplies perhaps, but nothing compared to what uninformed people think a person needs to set himself up in a money-paying enterprise.

True, the start will be small, but the initial success soon qual-

ifies you for the outside financing that builds your undertaking into
a giant. Such time-and-talent enterprises generally involve one of
three things:

- A service enterprise
- Commission sales
- Proprietary process

Service enterprises have launched some of America's biggest
success stories. H&R Block, the income tax specialist, is one example, the Berlitz language schools another. Tax preparation and personal instruction are just two examples of service specialties that
you can offer starting from scratch. Others include various business
services, temporary help agencies, home repairs, exterminating,
and interior decorating.

Commission sales can bring giant profits when you choose the
right specialty, such as art, stocks and bonds, real estate, antiques,
yachts, or even wheeling and dealing in businesses themselves by
forming a business brokerage.

A *proprietary process* is a fancy title for a business arrangement in which you own the title, or the copyright, or the patent to
a particular product or service. The money is made by granting
rights to others who want to use or produce what you have created.
The simplest example of this is the person who writes a book or a
song and then allows a publisher to produce it on a royalty basis.
Franchises work the same way; you develop a unique business plan
and then sell the rights to it. Also, inventors who sell their ideas to
big manufacturing firms are making money this way.

"But," you ask, "how can I get started with no cash and no loan
eligibility?" It's easy, if you choose the right product or service. Let
me tell you about Harry L., who cashed in on one of today's
fastest-growing hobbies—home computers.

Thousands of people have bought home computers, fascinated
by all the wonders they've heard computers can perform. But
many have soon found that it takes considerable knowledge and
ability in programming to get anything worthwhile out of a computer. They soon tire of the relatively few built-in games and programs.

And that's where Harry comes in. He was one of the earliest
computer hobbyists, and he naturally recognized that a computer

is just a piece of worthless plastic and metal unless it can be programmed.

So as soon as Harry saw that the computer hobby was catching on nationwide, he began to develop programs that could be used in the various brands of home computer. He put these programs on cassette tapes of the type that can be entered into any tape-equipped computer, and offered them for sale through computer stores and trade magazine ads.

As he expected, Harry's effort paid off handsomely. And as small business firms began to make use of computers, he began offering pre-packaged programs for them as well. His business, now grossing well into the millions of dollars, began with two things: his ability, and a dozen tape cassettes costing less than $35.

Cash in on Customer Financing

You've already read how Phil D. started a customer-financed business with his first newsletter. There are scores of other money-making methods in which the customers, in effect, buy your business for you.

Consider no-down-payment real estate. True, the financing comes from a bank or mortgage company (or the seller himself), but it is the customer (the person you rent the property to) who puts up the monthly mortgage payments.

I can hear you asking it now. "How can I obtain a mortgage with no loan eligibility?" Well, the truth is that the money is being loaned not on the basis of your personal ability to repay it, but on the projected income of the property. The lender has the real estate as collateral, and so is assured of getting his money back one way or another.

In a similar manner, contractors work with money supplied by their customers. The person who builds your house, decorates your office, landscapes your grounds, prepares your advertising, or manages your financial holdings, is actually working with your money. Such contractors receive reimbursements as they go, and many contracting fortunes have been built with virtually no personal investment.

Get Financing from Partners or Stockholders

You'll note that many entrepreneurs in this book (and many not in this book) begin with partners. Although partnerships do not always work out in the long run, they are an excellent means of obtaining start-up capital. The investment by your partner or partners can range from a small percentage all the way up to 100 percent.

But a partner who puts up 100 percent of the cash need not own even a controlling interest in the business. If you're a shrewd businessman, you'll retain the controlling interest. *Your* part of the investment is your business plan, your labor, and your know-how.

So here's a rule you should never violate:

Regardless of how badly you need outside investment capital from partners or stockholders, never grant someone else a controlling interest in your operation.

Note that I said *someone* else. If, instead of entering into a partnership, you sell stock publicly, it's usually possible to retain control with considerably less than half interest. That's because the other shares are held by a number of people, all of whom could never be expected to vote as a bloc. If you hold substantially more shares than any other stockholder, you should be able to maintain your grip on the company. And as you progress through this book you'll learn how to get millions in stock dollars without putting up any of your own cash.

How Control Is Retained

When Sam Wyly went into the business of performing computer services for other business firms, he put up $1,000 of his own cash and arranged to lease a computer to use in providing his service. To get that lease, he had to give up 49 percent interest in his own company. Not 51 percent, mind you, 49 percent. And he didn't let it remain at even that level for very long. Within four months, he bought back the 49 percent interest for $250,000. That's how rapidly his company had grown.

You'll be interested in knowing that Wyly even used credit in buying back the stock he'd put up to obtain the lease-type credit in the first place. In purchasing the $250,000 worth of shares, he put $5,000 down and agreed to pay the rest out of future profits.

Within six years of its launching, Sam Wyly's University Computing Company was grossing $100-million annually. His income tax alone amounted to $1-million.

Build Your Bankroll Through OJT

The old adage about killing two birds with one stone perfectly describes this method of getting your empire off the ground. OJT stands, of course, for on-the-job training—and it can build *two* bankrolls for you. One is in cash and the other is in valuable experience.

You may want to launch a type of business that requires a personal investment and you can see no way of obtaining the start-up money. There is a way, of course, and that is by taking a job with another company that is already involved in the line of work you've chosen. Your pay will be in the cash you need—and in a working *inside* knowledge of the field.

Marsha P. wanted to start a mail order business featuring gift items. Lacking the money for initial purchase of stock and advertising, she took the logical step of going to work for a mail order firm in her community.

"The best way of learning the specialized methods of the mail order business (or any other business) is to actually go to work in that field," Marsha points out. "The company I went to work for didn't sell gifts—it sold electronic gadgets—but many of the techniques are the same. I obtained a wealth of knowledge I couldn't have gotten otherwise—knowledge about such things as mailing lists, lettershops, ad preparation, drop-shipping, testing, and so forth."

The result is that, within less than a year, Marsha had earned enough cash to place her first ads and buy her starting stock—and enough experience to make a success of it. She quit her job, devoted herself full time to mail order, and built one of the nation's most successful gift specialty houses.

So, not having the needed cash or a way of getting it can actually be a boost to your wealth-building career. It can cause you to obtain the type of on-the-job training that helps you to move with more confidence and ability when the time does come to launch your own business.

SECOND RUNG:
USE OPM TO BUILD YOUR BUSINESS

Sooner or later (the sooner the better) you will begin using other people's money in financing the growth and development of your business. And you will continue to use OPM throughout your business career, as I've noted earlier in this chapter. For, if leverage can do wonders for you when you have just a few dollars to invest, think of what it can do after you've built up your net worth a bit. The more you make, the more you have to leverage, and when you reach the big time your leveraging can really hit giant strides.

Kemmons Wilson, the Holiday Inn founder, has always used leverage. In fact, he tells his friends he never wanted to *own* a million dollars, he wanted to *owe* it. And by owing *millions* of dollars, his enterprise has reached the *billion*-dollar category.

His leveraging began with a $50 loan that he agreed to repay at the rate of a dollar a week. The loan was for a popcorn machine that he installed in a neighborhood movie house. You know the rest of his story, having read it in Chapter 2. You know that one undertaking led to another, including pinball and vending machines, housing, motels, and then diversification into other industries.

But let me explain how leveraging played an important role in each step along the way. After building a home, he borrowed to expand his vending machine route, and then he obtained rental real estate properties for 10 percent down.

He reached the point where he was able to borrow about one-third of a million dollars to build his first motel. The leveraging became more sophisticated when he began to franchise his motels. This meant that his franchisees, not he, paid for the construction and start-up costs, with Wilson's firm getting a cut of the proceeds. And, of course, stock sales have played an important role in the empire's expansion.

The Warnings Are Not for You

Most traditional articles and books on business warn of getting in too deeply too soon. And, to an extent, they're right. But such pieces are written for people who merely want to start "a business"—not those who aim to build million-dollar empires.

They warn that most business failures are caused by undercapitalization, which means the owners didn't have enough money to carry them through the early getting-established period. This won't happen to you if you follow the advice in this book. You'll be taking one step at a time and testing each new step before it is taken. Never will you jump into the ocean until you've tested its temperature with first your toe, then your leg, and then your arms as well.

When a plan has been tested and you're convinced it will work, you can borrow with confidence. And, incidentally, that will keep you from ever having to be under-capitalized.

But keep this firmly in mind:

You cannot become rich without OPM. The sooner you are able to use it, the faster your fortune will be built.

True, you might become a movie star or record a hit song and become rich. But what good is great acting or singing talent without a means of presenting it to an audience? So you see, even famous performers benefit from OPM—the money that has been invested in the showcases that bring their talent to the public. And you can bet that money advisors to the talented-rich make sure their clients leverage their earnings to make even more money for them.

Success Breeds Success in Borrowing, Too

The first reason for using OPM as early as possible is that it gives you a bigger start than would otherwise be possible. But an important second reason is this:

You immediately begin to build a business credit record.

Establishing a good credit record in business means that *more* money will become available to you sooner. And remember that you'll be using credit as long as you are in business.

Even well-to-do people who never go into business need good credit records. You may have heard the story of the millionaire's son who applied for a department store charge account, wanting it so he could buy things without having to carry a lot of cash with him. He had never borrowed money and thus had no credit record. He was turned down, and yet he could probably afford to buy the department store!

Peter Kanavos learned early that success breeds success in borrowing. He needed $46,000 to buy a tavern. Not having any resources of his own (his father, a Greek immigrant, was dead, and Peter had worked his way through college), he knew that banks would not stake him. So what did he do? He borrowed the *resources* that would convince the banks to lend him money.

He borrowed from friends, former teachers, ex-employers, and so forth—$1,000 here, $2,000 there. He obtained $31,000 that way. With that money in hand, he could then approach a bank, and was granted a $15,000 loan to round out his start-up investment.

The tavern did well, and Mr. Kanavos used the Success Repetition Factor. He opened up more bars and some liquor stores as well.

A Giant Credit Standing

Just as Kemmons Wilson switched to real estate from another field, so did Peter Kanavos. Apartment buildings led to industrial parks and commercial developments. Leveraging all the way, he rapidly became a multi-millionaire. He built a giant credit standing for himself, and used it well in projects located throughout the Boston area.

A similar story can be told about a European immigrant named Peter Hurst. He was visiting Jackson, Michigan, shortly after arriving in the U.S., and he encountered some local businessmen in a hotel there.

Hurst told them of his dream: manufacturing industrial hosing that would be flexible and would have detachable fittings, a feature not commonly available. He planned to go to New York City to obtain financing and start his company. But the Jackson businessmen were impressed with Peter Hurst; so much so that ten of them offered to put up a thousand dollars each if he would stay in Jackson. He accepted, and thus was born the Aeroquip Corporation. Other leveraging came with the mortgage obtained for the purchase of an old factory building. And with this backing, Aeroquip soon became a multi-million-dollar operation.

How to Attract Outside Cash to Your Venture

Whether or not you have a nest egg in the bank to help you get started, there are a number of outside money-sources that may be open to you:

1. Personal loans
2. Collateral loans
3. Business loans
4. Leasing

5. Credit from suppliers
6. Small Business Administration
7. Small Business Investment Companies

You've already seen how some of these methods have been used in the experiences of the SMMs you've met so far in this book. You'll see the other methods in action as you progress through the book. But you can benefit by understanding these methods of financing right now. As we examine each individually, think of how it can be used to underwrite your own business plans.

Personal Loans

If you haven't already borrowed to the hilt on your personal credit rating, ready cash may be available to you from banks, finance companies, credit unions, credit card companies, and friends and relatives.

Personal loans are just what the name implies—made to you, personally, on the basis of your credit standing. Projected business profits are not taken into account.

If you examine your monthly statement from one of the major credit card companies, you may find that you are eligible for "cash advances" of several hundred or even several thousand dollars. Similarly, many banks offer "ready reserve" checking accounts allowing you to overdraw up to a set limit which could be as much as $5,000.

If you've made unsecured loans from a bank before and repaid them on time you should be eligible for another one now. One businessman I know used this unorthodox method: He took out a modest loan from the bank and did nothing with the money, but used it to *pay back the loan* well ahead of schedule. A month or so later, he took out a larger loan from the same bank, and did the same thing. He repeated the process again, with an even larger loan. Finally, when he wanted a truly sizable sum for a business plan he had in mind, the bank gladly provided him with the money on the basis of the excellent record he had established.

Personal, unsecured loans usually carry a higher interest rate than other kinds of lending. But if your business plan is a good one, the power of leverage can far outstrip the extra cost of the loan.

Collateral Loans

You've probably taken out collateral loans before, perhaps when you bought your last car, and almost certainly when you bought your home. Your home may now have increased in value and this, combined with the fact that you've paid off some of the principal, may enable you to increase your mortgage.

If you have funds in a savings account that you don't want to touch, you can get a passbook loan at relatively low interest, while continuing to earn interest on your savings. Loans can also be obtained on other items of value that you own, such as stock or insurance policies.

Business Loans

Generally you have to have a proven business record in order to obtain a business loan from a bank. But even at the outset it's worth trying for because of one distinct advantage: You pay what is known as *simple interest*. In many other types of loans, you repay the principal, plus interest, on a monthly basis. Thus you don't have full use of the money for the full period of the loan, even though you must pay interest as if you did.

With a typical business loan, you borrow a lump sum and pay back the lump sum when the term has expired. You have full use of the money for the entire period. That can substantially cut your interest cost.

Leasing

If your business is one that requires expensive equipment, property, or buildings, give serious thought to leasing instead of buying. You can lease anything from a drill press to acres of land. In between are virtually everything you'll need in the operation of your business, including office equipment, cars, trucks, even furnishings and computers. Leasing is a pay-as-you-go deal. No large down payment is needed. The arrangement allows you to deduct the entire cost on your income tax returns, instead of merely the depreciation that is allowed on equipment you own.

Credit from Suppliers

If yours is to be a business featuring the sale of products, the companies that supply you with those products may be persuaded to allow credit of up to 90 days and sometimes even more. Many is the firm that uses such credit to the hilt.

And equipment you intend to keep can usually be purchased on time, either through the supplier or as collateral for a loan from another source.

Small Business Administration

Can't find money elsewhere? The Small Business Administration run by the federal government can be a "last resort" helper. In some cases it makes a full, direct loan. In others, it makes up the difference between what a bank will lend and what you need.

Whether or not you do borrow through the SBA, you should make use of its other services, which include business counseling by its own experts and by active and retired businessmen who have volunteered their services. Write to the Small Business Administration, Washington, D.C. 20416, for the address of the office nearest you.

Small Business Investment Companies

SBICs are groups of private investors interested in making direct loans to small enterprises. They were created by federal legislation to encourage the flow of funds to businesses showing good potential.

These funds are called risk capital, and it may cost you more to borrow than some other types of financing. The extra cost could be in the form of consultant or service fees, or the SBIC you deal with might require some equity in your firm (meaning a partial stock interest.)

The Small Business Administration can put you in touch with the SBIC that might be of help to you.

Don't Overlook This Possibility

This listing doesn't include stock sales because that was mentioned earlier, but please bear in mind that it can be the easiest way to obtain full-scale starting capital without any personal risk. It's entirely possible to obtain *millions of dollars* in start-up capital through stock sales—without putting up any dollars yourself. Chapter 12 gives greater detail of this million-dollar fortune-building method.

THIRD RUNG: EMPLOY THE "SCALE TECHNIQUE"

A highly effective method of building a giant industry is to launch it on a small scale and then expand the scale as profits and financing allow. You'd be amazed at how small the starting scale can be, and still lead to outstanding success.

The scale can be as small as picking a product and then selling it to friends. That's what a station agent at the express office in Redwood, Minnesota, did with a shipment of watches he obtained. His fellow agents bought out his supply, and he bought more watches, selling them as well. Before long, he quit his job and devoted full time to selling watches through the mail, gradually adding other products. Richard Sears thus launched the firm now known as Sears Roebuck.

After you have launched your business, even on a very small scale, never forget your goal: the empire you plan to build. Unlike the average small business, your first undertaking is the means, not the end.

Thus, every move is made with the idea of the growth and expansion that you have in mind. Many businesses have expansion factors already built in. Phil D.'s line of work—publishing newsletters—is an example. There's no limit to the number he, or anyone, can publish provided the staff can obtain the information needed by business subscribers.

Arthur N.'s real estate holdings are another example. With continued good use of leverage, there is no limit to how much his holdings can increase.

Here's an important piece of advice, passed on to me by a man who got his start with a greatly scaled-down version of the big business he ultimately planned to build. He achieved his goal by adhering to this rule:

> **From the beginning, look toward operating a business that can eventually be run on a day-to-day basis by its employees. This allows you to concentrate more on growth than on minor details. Know from the beginning *how* you will grow. A regional or nationwide network of branches? Or steady expansion of your central facility? Either way, once the initial operation is functioning smoothly, concentrate your efforts on the future.**

Thus, if you plan, a year from now, to have a sizable trucking fleet, don't build a garage that will house just the one vehicle you may now have. Better to rent space until you can afford to put up a building of adequate size. And don't spend your time sweeping the floor in your first store when you should really be out looking for new floors to sweep.

Speed Your Growth Through Profit Plow-Back

Plowing back your early profits for expansion purposes is a must when you're starting with zero cash or little more than that. If you sincerely want to become a millionaire, you won't be tempted to put the first profits into, say, your family's vacation budget.

The small businessman who is satisfied with his little corner store can afford to use profits for a trip to Aspen or Europe. He has no other need for his money. But you are a far more ambitious person. As a future SMM, you know that good *business* use of today's money will provide a lot more pleasure-money in the future. Right now, you're living for tomorrow, not today.

Smart fortune builders establish a growth fund as soon as they possibly can. You should do the same. If you don't need your early business income to live on, use it for your enterprise to grow on. A side benefit is that re-investing can often cut down on income tax payments. In a sense, Uncle Sam thus becomes your partner instead of your creditor. Proper business use of your early profits will make the next rung up the ladder much easier to reach.

FOURTH RUNG:
USE THE SUCCESS REPETITION FACTOR

By now you are familiar with what I call the Success Repetition Factor. You've seen it work for a number of SMMs whose stories I've already passed on to you, and you'll see it work in many other examples still to be given in this book.

But let me tell you right now about Clara J., who brought her enterprise up from virtually nothing.

You've heard of "Mom and Pop" grocery stores. Well, Clara started a Mom store. There was no Pop, because she was a widow, living above what had been her late husband's electrical repair shop. Not knowing how to fix even a toaster, Clara naturally had to close the shop upon her husband's death. His tools weren't worth much, but selling them gave her enough money to put up some shelves in the shop and stock the shelves with canned goods.

She bought an old refrigeration unit to hold frozen foods on one side and chilled goods such as milk and cheese on the other. Then she opened her doors to the public.

Her visualization had enabled her to know the plan would work, because the store was in a well-traveled location and she knew that so-called convenience food stores had been profitable elsewhere. Customers readily pay higher prices for staple foods when the store is located "just around the corner" and they don't have to drive to the supermarket.

Profits from that store enabled Clara to rent another vacant store for a second outlet, and a third. And then she was able to borrow money to *build* convenience food stores at strategic locations. The upshot is that she now has a chain of 30 stores in a 10-county area. She is a millionaire businesswoman.

You should make a point of reviewing the Success Repetition Factor as explained throughout the first two chapters of this book, and the specific instructions given in Chapter 7. Read how to build a success and then repeat it again and again. Put into action the time-proven fact that achieving one success provides you with the confidence, ability, and recognition that will allow you to do it repeatedly, on an ever-growing scale.

4

How to Spot and Cash In on Million-Dollar Opportunities

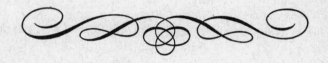

Can *anyone* become a millionaire? Yes, if he or she truly wants to. Take it from J. Paul Getty, who was described by Fortune Magazine as "the richest man in America" and by other publications as the richest man in the world.

J. Paul Getty said, about becoming a millionaire, if you want to you can—"if you are able to recognize the limitless opportunities and potentials around you."

And that is exactly what this chapter is about—not only recognizing, but cashing in on the million-dollar opportunities that surround you.

HOW TO CAPITALIZE ON YOUR ABILITIES AND EXPERIENCE

A listener to one of my radio broadcasts called me one day after I had used the quote from J. Paul Getty that you've just read. The young man said to me, "It was easy for J. Paul Getty to say there are opportunities all around you, but it's not so easy for me, a poor working guy, to *find* them!"

I informed the young man that the first place to look for opportunity was in his job. A great many SMMs, I explained, have found their million-dollar ideas in the course of a workday, laboring for somebody else.

He snickered. "Sure, if they work as an executive for a giant corporation. Do you know where *I* work? In the back of a fast food establishment, cooking hamburgers. Now you find me a million dollars there!"

"Have you ever heard of Jerry Gordon?" I asked. He replied that he hadn't. I said, "Let me tell you about him. He, too, worked as a cook in fast food establishments. One day, while working in a Kentucky Fried Chicken Store in Oklahoma, he noticed that the flour used in their products was being sifted by hand. When he thought about it, it amazed him. Here he was, in one of modern-day America's most successful fast food stores, and they were still sifting flour *by hand!* He took a piece of scrap paper and drew a sketch of a motor-driven sifter."

I continued, "As soon as he got a chance, he took that sketch to a sheet metal company and had a prototype made up for him—on credit. He agreed to pay the company the $194 cost after he succeeded in selling the product to the Kentucky Fried Chicken chain."

Sell it to the chain he did. As I told the young man who had phoned me, "He took his prototype to Harland Sanders, the Kentucky Colonel himself. The colonel bought 12 of them, cash in advance, and then suggested that Jerry show his product at an upcoming KFC convention. He did, driving to the convention city in a broken-down pickup truck that somehow got him from Tulsa to Chicago. And it was good that he made it, because the owners of KFC stores attending the convention loved the idea of not having to sift flour by hand anymore.

"Colonel Sanders loved the idea, too, and decided to help Jerry form his own manufacturing corporation. He loaned the young man $10,000 and promised that once the money was paid back, the concern would be entirely Jerry's. He did pay the Colonel back within 18 months, and that was the start of a multi-million-dollar operation that went on to make and sell food-processing products as well as other items designed to save time and money for business."

There was a brief silence at the other end of the telephone line. Then the young men said, "Hmm. Well, I guess I'll just have to keep a sharper eye out."

YOUR JOB CAN BE YOUR FORTUNE

You've probably heard it said many times that it's next to impossible to become rich working for somebody else, and it's true. But your job—no matter what type of job it is—can provide you with:

- Ideas for filling an important need
- Training and experience
- Valuable personal contacts

It could take years of study to obtain the wealth-building potential you already have because of your work background. Let's take *your* job and see how these three assets—ideas, experience, and contacts—can be the launchpad of your own million-dollar enterprise.

MILLION-DOLLAR IDEAS RIGHT WHERE YOU WORK

Find a nagging problem where you work and chances are that the same type of problem exists in all similar establishments. Jerry Gordon's problem was sifting flour by hand, and that created his million-dollar idea.

Walter Botthof's problem was not really his own, but one he encountered frequently while working as an advertising man, representing a group of newspapers. He noticed that many advertisers had accumulated bulky files and reams of material on the advertising rates and circulation figures of publications across the United States.

To help them a bit, Botthof compiled a list of price and circulation figures for the papers he represented, compared with those of his papers' competitors. Advertisers found it a big help, and he soon realized that if there were to be a nationwide listing of all such figures, advertisers would no longer have to send away to each individual publication requesting the information and then perhaps wait months for it to arrive.

Thus was born Standard Rate and Data Service, published from a small second story loft. If you've ever had anything to do with advertising, you know that it is now the "bible" of the industry. It serves thousands of subscribers and has become the basis of a multi-million-dollar operation.

Every line of work has its share of unsolved problems. They remain unsolved because people have come to accept them as unavoidable. It takes a Jerry Gordon or Walter Botthof, or *you*, to find a solution and profit from it. And usually the solutions are so simple that co-workers say, "Gee, why didn't *I* think of that?" They didn't think of it because they weren't looking.

A MILLION DOLLARS WORTH OF EXPERIENCE

No matter whether you work as a short order cook, a parts man in an auto shop, a bank teller, or a sales clerk, you have gained experience that can prove immensely valuable to you. You might call it on-the-job training, or OJT in your preparation for millionairehood. It certainly has proven so for many others.

Consider this fact:

A great many self-made millionaires have built their fortunes after learning the ropes in a so-called routine job.

It can be an ironic twist. Think of the many thousands of dollars spent to send young people to college to prepare them for a lifetime of wage-earning. Then think of the SMMs (many of whom never went to college) who *were paid* for their money-making education—paid by reporting to work in jobs that that would lead to their independent careers.

Answer these questions:

- Would Jerry Gordon ever have devised the motorized flour sifter if he hadn't worked as a short order cook?
- Would Walter Botthof have dreamed up Standard Rate and Data Service if he hadn't worked as an advertising salesman?

And what about Nolan Bushnell, whose varied experience had included working in an amusement park and training in electronics? He combined the two, and with a partner he invested $500 in 1972 to form a company known as Atari, Inc.

Bushnell's amusement park work had shown him what kinds of attractions people in the 1970's were going for, and his electronics training enabled him to devise a product he was sure they would like. He was right. Atari became the manufacturer of *Pong* and other video games. Sales quickly climbed into the millions-of-dollars range, and four years after he founded it, Bushnell sold the company for $28 million.

The wealth-building knowledge you are gaining in this book will help you find the tremendous profit opportunities open to you because of your own work experience. You already know, for example, that:

- Opportunities exist in all kinds of work
- You can get your biggest ideas from routine problems
- You don't need a lot of money to get started
- You can reach the million-dollar level in short order

Now let's delve into the third benefit of basing your money project on your work experience.

A MILLION DOLLARS WORTH OF CONTACTS

Let's say that John Jones takes a vocational course in spray-painting, while Jim Smith learns it working in an auto body shop. And let's say that after six months both men are equally skilled at painting cars. Which person do you think has, at this point, the best potential for devising his own business plan and succeeding at it? Everything else being equal, Jim Smith does. He's no more capable than John Jones, and he's had no more actual paint-spraying experience, but he's made *contacts*. In his OJT, he has:

- Dealt with customers and learned their complaints
- Met the product salesmen who visit his shop
- Learned from co-workers and his boss

In other words, Jim Smith has not only learned the physical technique of painting a car, he's learned a lot of the business details that go with it—and he's made contacts in the business. Thus, if he were to set up his own shop he would:

- Know what customers are looking for
- Know where to obtain his supplies
- Know where to look for employees and whom to hire

This is a simplified illustration of what work contacts can do for you. Such contacts have proven to be of great advantage to many budding SMMs. Wasn't it Joe Hrudka, mentioned in Chapter 2, who first learned of the overheated gasket problem from the speed shops where he'd worked, and wasn't it he who sold his first prototype to one of those shops? You can be sure his early contacts were important in getting him started in the business that quickly made him a multi-millionaire.

COMBINE IDEAS, EXPERIENCE, AND CONTACTS TO MAKE A FORTUNE

You can see why I always advise people to look first to their employment backgrounds when seeking to enter business for themselves. It's because in launching a project stemming from what you've learned on the job:

- You deal with ideas you know will work
- You've had experience that would be expensive and time-consuming to duplicate
- You are familiar with the unique problems and conditions of the industry
- You have encountered people who can be of tremendous help to you in the future

John Garrett built up quite a valuable business education for himself when he worked for several large aviation companies over a nine-year period. During that time, he became particularly skilled at procuring hard-to-locate parts and tools. So skilled, in fact, that he decided to step out on his own and form a supply company serving aircraft manufacturers in southern California.

That was the start of his empire-building process, and you can be sure the ideas, experience, and contacts he'd gained during nine years as an employee stood him in good stead.

One of the ideas he had was for pressurizing aircraft cabins.

Up until then, the only pressurization was available by means of oxygen masks—these were all right for fighter pilots but certainly not for paying passengers on luxury airliners.

So Garrett created the AiResearch Division of his company, and it helped develop the equipment that enables large aircraft to fly at higher altitudes and thus at faster speeds. AiResearch products are used in most major airliners today, thanks to the ideas, experience, and contacts John Garrett made while working for others.

The moral:

The million-dollar opportunity you seek, and the means of cashing in on it, can be as close as your 9-to-5 job.

Now let's see how and why that opportunity can become your million-dollar meal ticket.

HOW TO SOLVE A PROBLEM AND MAKE A MINT

Regardless of what work you do, each day you are solving problems. Most of them are small, routine annoyances, and you deal with them in a routine fashion. Occasionally, you may come up with a unique solution to a particularly bothersome problem and you pass your solution along to your superiors. Your solution may even become standard operating procedure in your line of work.

Some bigger companies even give awards for such solutions. People who've dropped notes in these companies' idea boxes walk away with fifty dollars or even a few thousand dollars.

But here's a point worth remembering:

Problems that exist in your place of employment probably exist in most similar establishments. You can make big money by finding a solution and then selling that solution to other companies.

The solution can be in the form of a product, such as Jerry Gordon's flour-sifter. Or it can be in the form of a service, such as Walter Botthof's Standard Rate and Data Service.

Think about it for a minute. What if Jerry Gordon had merely gone home and made a flour-sifter to use in the store where he worked? And what if Walter Botthof had confined himself to a small listing of the publications in the area he represented? Both men would have missed out on million-dollar opportunities.

But they didn't miss out on the opportunities, because each man recognized his idea's value not only in his own job—but in making the work of many other people easier and more efficient. Jerry Gordon knew that *all* KFC stores could use flour-sifters, and Walter Botthof knew that *all* advertisers needed a single source for comparing advertising figures.

FOLLOW THIS "PROBLEM-TO-FORTUNE" FORMULA

Here, then, are the steps to take in solving a problem and building a fortune:

1. Determine if the problem is faced by similar establishments elsewhere.
2. Work out the solution in detail, but be quiet about it.
3. When the solution has been put on paper, determine how it can be duplicated for the use of all companies requiring it.
4. Arrange for whatever initial financing may be required and then offer your solution for sale.

This, essentially, is the procedure followed by the Gordons, Botthofs, and all of the other SMMs who developed giant money projects stemming from their work experience.

Let's take a slightly closer look at each of the four steps.

1. **Similar establishments:** There are probably hundreds, perhaps thousands, of other firms across the land very similar to the one where you work. All face the same problems you face. Word travels fast; if your problem had been solved eslewhere, your firm would probably know about it. But it's a good idea to read all the trade journals in your field that you can get hold of. This will give you a better picture of industry-wide problems and what is—or what is not—being done about them.

2. **Detailed solution:** It's not good enough to work out the solution in your head. Prepare a prototype, which in the

case of a product would be a working model, and in the case of a service would be a system of operation. It's important to keep quiet about it, because if your product or system is put to use where you work, it can then become the property of that company. Or it can become "public domain," ready for any company to adopt at will.

3. **Duplication:** Your product or service may or may not be of the type that should be patented or copyrighted. In the case of products, chances are that somebody else, years ago, patented a similar item—but it was never put to the particular use you have in mind. Thus, if you are the first to use it this way, you have a great head start over others who will eventually try to imitate your success. In any event, determine how you can make the product or service available for all who want to buy it.

4. **Financing and sale:** Initial financing for the prototype (in Jerry Gordon's case, $194) need not involve much money. The real financing need will come after you have received definite indications that your item is salable. Going into production is what costs money, and you should apply one of the loan or partnership techniques outlined in the previous chapter. Then—full speed ahead!

Convert Your Job Into a Business

You may not even need a brilliant idea to earn a million dollars on the basis of your work experience. You may not even have to solve any unique problems. Instead, you can do this:

Rather than work for somebody else's company, work for yourself by selling your service to many companies.

By doing the very work you are performing now (and eventually hiring others to do the same thing) you can make much more than if you were to continue doing it for a salary.

That, in effect, is what John Garrett did when he left the Douglas Aircraft Company. In his job for that firm, he had become proficient in locating hard-to-get tools and parts. It was natural for him to use that proficiency in setting up the Garrett Supply Co. and perform the same work for many aircraft manufacturers. Garrett Supply became the Garrett Corporation, and that, in turn, was the parent of the AiResearch Manufacturing Division.

This same kind of transition has taken place in all kinds of work. Here are some examples:

- Secretaries establish their own secretarial service agencies.
- Former policemen launch detective and guard agencies.
- Real estate salesmen open their own brokerage firms.
- Engineers open firms to do contract work.
- Accountants open public accounting offices.
- Bartenders establish bartender agencies.
- Teachers open private schools.

The list could be practically endless, but you get the idea. You may wonder, however, why companies often prefer to hire services from outside agencies rather than have their own employees do the work. There are several reasons:

1. They can save money when there is not enough of a particular kind of work to require a full-time employee.
2. They also save money by not having to pay employee benefits such as unemployment compensation, Social Security, pensions, hospitalization, etc.
3. They avoid personnel problems when dealing with an outside agency rather than an internal employee.
4. Whether it's actual or not, they expect more professional work from a professional agency than they might get from "one of their own."

I can sense that you have another question. "O.K.," you say, "I can see that customers benefit from hiring my services, but how do *I* benefit? Why not keep on working for one company, with all the security that provides, instead of seeking work from several? After all, I can only do so much work."

And therein, my friend, lies the answer. First of all, your "job security" may not be nearly as great as you think. (Take a look at all the layoffs and squeeze-outs that occur every day.) But more important, consider this vital fact:

Working as an employee allows you to earn only as much money as your individual effort is worth. But when you form

a company, you profit from the work of *many* employees.

Thus, if you were, for example, to leave your job as a travel agent and open your own agency, you'd get a cut of *all* the commissions earned by people working for you. Or if you were to start a secretarial service, you'd get a slice of the pay earned by all of the secretaries working in your agency. Thus, the amount of money you can make is limited only by the need for the service you sell.

LEARN NEW WAYS OF MAKING BIG MONEY

The greatest part of this chapter has been devoted to finding big money opportunities in your work experience because that's where I always advise people to look first. But sometimes an opportunity you spot is not related to any work experience you've had, and such an opportunity might be too good to pass up.

Let's go back to the early part of this century when a young man—a glove salesman—walked into a nickelodeon and was enthused by the simple motion picture he saw. In fact, he saw more than a motion picture. He saw an entertainment potential that needed developing. Thus, trained only in the glove business and having had no experience at all in show business, Samuel Goldwyn decided to switch careers.

It wasn't that Goldwyn was unhappy with selling gloves. He was making an excellent salary doing it. And it wasn't that he merely wanted to switch careers. A friend advised him of a great opportunity—peddling tamales, which were selling like . . . well, like tamales . . . on the west coast but had not yet caught on in the east.

But Sam Goldwyn didn't want to sell gloves *or* tamales. He wanted to get into motion pictures, where he saw a truly brilliant future. And of course he found it.

There *is* a time when you should consider non-job-related business opportunities. That time comes when:

1. You spot an outstanding opportunity.
2. The opportunity appears greater than any related to your work experience.

You *can* go into a new business cold. You can either undergo a crash training program, or you can get experts to help you as partners, employees, or on a contract basis.

Sam Goldwyn did it by signing up vaudeville producer Jesse Lasky and actor-writer Cecil B. DeMille as partners. His business acumen and their show business experience formed the perfect combination to meet the challenges of what was then a great new opportunity.

Great new opportunities continue to this day. Just a few years ago, as you read earlier in this chapter, Nolan Bushnell spotted the opportunity for video games, and he sparked the growth of a giant new industry.

Right now—today—home computers still provide a great new opportunity and you can be sure that entrepreneurs have jumped onto the band wagon. Great new opportunities will always exist, because each new technological development brings with it greater requirements for new products and services.

Using your money-project notebook as outlined in Chapter 2 may have already led you to some of these opportunities. Continued use of it with the business knowledge you are gaining as you progress through this book will almost certainly do so.

What, then, do you *do* when you spot an opportunity in a field that is foreign to you? You learn the field. As fast as you can.

OJT FOR MILLIONAIRES

The best way to learn any business field is to work in it. If you are in the position of being able to switch jobs to take one that will give you practical experience, all to the good. If you must continue in your present job while you learn the new field, then you can get your on-the-job training on a part-time basis.

One man who took OJT on a full-time basis was Harry Rosenfeld, who was to become a millionaire dress manufacturer, producing "class market dresses" at mass market prices. He spotted a great opportunity in the dress field and envisioned a method of providing high fashion at prices that could be paid by women who normally shopped in bargain basements.

He got his OJT by taking a job at one of the lowest levels of an established firm and learning as many aspects of the business as he could before starting on his own. He was paid for his training—and that training paid him back handsomely.

But perhaps you can't afford to quit your job until your business project is well established. You may have a family to support, a mortgage to pay. You still have these alternatives:

- Take a part-time job in the field you've chosen.
- Start a spare-time business in the field.
- Sign up a knowledgeable partner.
- Take special training courses.
- "Hire" the needed expertise.

Each of these five methods has been used by SMMs to get them started building their fortunes. Here are some instances from my files:

- Harold F. spotted an opportunity for providing low-cost "canned" music for restaurants. In many establishments he frequented, the restaurants played FM radios for background music, and the commercials and newscasts were annoying. On the other hand, traditional "piped-in" music was too expensive for many small establishments. Harold's idea was to provide tape players and tapes at half the usual monthly fee. He got his training by working nights and weekends for a traditional background music firm serving his area.

- Irv K. spotted the need for a land-clearing business in his fast-growing area. Knowing nothing about work with heavy equipment, he took on the foreman of an existing firm as his partner, and together they have forged a highly lucrative company.

- Sam T. recognized the need for a good electronics store in his neighborhood, but he knew next to nothing about the field. So he took several comprehensive home study courses and also signed up for a business course at the local community college. When the time came to open his store, he was fully trained for it—and for the string of branches that followed.

- Helen B. knew that a shopper's newspaper would win instant acceptance in her area, but she knew nothing about

printing or publishing. From the start, she hired the expertise by farming out the typesetting, printing, and distribution functions. Now most of the production is done in the
central plant that her early profits enabled her to build, and
she's planning other editions of her paper for outlying areas.

HOW TO READ THE SIGNALS THAT SPELL SUCCESS

Once your mind is tuned to making money, success signals can
and will appear from the least expected places. The truth is, these
signals always exist, *but only now are you equipped to recognize
them.* Little incidents that might have meant nothing to you a year
ago now take on new significance—important money-making significance.

Sam Goldwyn was enthralled when he saw his first nickelodeon show, and he saw that the other members of the audience
were also. Up to that time, movies were used merely as between-
acts features at vaudeville performances. From the audience's reaction, Goldwyn saw that movies could become the *main* attraction.

Ralph Schneider forgot his wallet when he took some business
associates out to dinner in New York. Embarrassed and unable to
pay the check, he put in an emergency call to his wife to bail him
out. That experience led him to begin thinking of a means by which
people could pay for food under a universal charge system, say a
charge card. And thus was born the Diners Club.

Ray Kroc was peddling malted milk mixers when he became
intrigued by the fact that a little restaurant in California had purchased eight of his machines. He went out to the place run by the
two McDonald brothers and saw why they needed so many
mixers—they were doing a land-office business. He tried to convince them to open up branches so he could sell them more
machines. They weren't interested—but they did agree to give him
the right to franchise their restaurants on his own. Thus the giant
McDonald's chain came into being, and Ray Kroc made his first Big
MacMillion.

Robert Petersen had always been a hot rod enthusiast. He
even thought of starting a magazine geared for hot rodders. But the
event that signalled success to him was a three-day hot rod show in
Los Angeles, attended by 42,000 persons. If there was such wide-

spread interest in hot rods in LA, it existed all across the land. Not everyone could attend shows, but all could read the *Hot Rod* magazine he was to found. It was the first of a string of many special interest magazines that made Robert Petersen a millionaire.

Richard Knerr and Spud Melin were two college buddies who shared the hobby of training falcons to hunt. One method was to dispatch small meatballs at the flying birds, using a slingshot. While trying to sell a bird to a prospect they noticed that he took more interest in the slingshot than in the falcon. In fact, he said he wouldn't buy the bird but he would purchase the slingshot. The boys spotted this as a success signal if there ever was one, and they began manufacturing slingshots in a garage. One success led to another, and they've become rich creating such things as the Hula Hoop, the Frisbee Flying Saucer, and the Super Ball.

A Surefire Success Signal

Of course, the *best* signal of success is a plan that has already been tried and proven by somebody else. And it's hardly ever too late for you to jump on the bandwagon and perhaps do even better than those who preceded you. You'll learn all about this in the next chapter.

5

Utilize the Secrets of Self-Made Millionaires

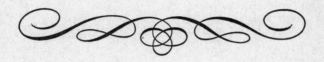

Would you take your lifesavings, buy a brand new automobile, and then proceed to tear it apart? A young railroad mechanic did that, and it led to his becoming rich.

Walter Chrysler tore his car apart not merely to see how it worked, but to see how he could design and build cars from scratch. With only a correspondence course as prior training, Chrysler became a giant in the automotive industry—his firm rising to become one of the big three.

Walter Chrysler was a creative copycat. The purpose of this chapter is to show why you should be one, too.

BE A "CREATIVE COPYCAT" AND GET RICH

Why not base your success on a formula tried and proven by others? Many people have the mistaken belief that most self-made millionaires got where they are by being innovators—geniuses who've come up with new inventions, new business systems, or fantastic new ideas. The truth is that few SMMs were first in their field.

Instead, most entrepreneurs spot what others are successful at and then set out to do the same, or perhaps a little better. The operations of most businesses are an open book to anyone with an observant eye.

Just as Walter Chrysler tore that car apart so *he* could learn how to make cars (and improve on what was then being made) you can earn a fortune learning and using the proven techniques of today's most successful millionaires.

MADE-TO-ORDER SUCCESS

Too many people spend a lifetime daydreaming and waiting for "the big idea" to hit them when, all the while, big ideas surround them, waiting to be tapped. Every time you walk into a store, read an ad, sign a check, pass a billboard, or read a newspaper, a big idea is staring you in the face. At one time it may have been somebody else's exclusive idea, but now it's there for anybody to profit from.

The story is told about a young executive in a firm that had a growing chain of hamburger stands. This ambitious young man went to the president of his company with what he thought was a bright idea. He suggested that they set up a research department to determine how they could make their product even more appealing to the public. The boss told him in no uncertain terms that the only research they needed was to send somebody out to a McDonald's for a hamburger. All they needed to know was inside that hamburger.

Macy's may not tell Gimbel's but you can be sure the two stores watch each other very closely. Aaron Montgomery Ward may have started the first mail order house in the United States, but you can be sure that there were a number of other entrepreneurs close on his heels. Frank Woolworth, may have opened the first variety store, but J.C. Penney wasn't far behind.

USE YOUR MENTAL MICROSCOPE AND GET RICH

Rare is the successful businessman who's going to let you pore over his financial records, but the signs of outstanding success are easy enough to spot. And so are the methods employed to achieve that success. With just a little bit of effort, here's what you can learn about practically any successful company:

- What it does to attract customers
- Its most successful selling methods
- The type of people it sells to
- How much it charges
- What goes into its product or service
- The locations it finds best for its stores or offices
- Its customer policies

And this is just a partial list of the things you can learn about a business operation in a completely legal and honorable manner; no Watergate burglars needed. In fact, let me tell you how one young woman did it.

Dorothy G. was interested in writing, and then selling by mail, a home study course in handicrafts. In the seven business criteria listed above, here's what she learned:

Attracting customers: Dorothy went to the library and delved into the back issues of hundreds of magazines, taking notes on all the ads she could find for home study courses. She learned that few courses are sold directly from the ad; instead, the advertisement invites the reader to send for descriptive literature.

Successful selling methods: Next, she sent postcards to dozens of correspondence schools, not only in the field she had chosen, but those offering other courses as well. She examined and compared the sales literature they sent her, and soon learned that many firms follow up that literature with a series of subsequent mailings to each prospect.

Type of clientele: Not seeking a business that deals directly with the public, Dorothy couldn't stand outside a store and watch customers come and go to determine the type of people the firm sells to. What she could and did do was make note of the type of magazines in which the correspondence schools advertised. This told her a lot about the people toward whom they were directing their advertising.

How much is charged: As with any publicly offered product, this was easy to determine from the sales literature. What came as a surprise to Dorothy was that a number of firms, in their follow-up letters, offered price reductions of one form or another.

What goes into the product: Dorothy bought several courses—three in her chosen field and two in other fields—and got a wealth of knowledge about the course materials, how they were put together, and their methods of teaching.

Locations of stores or offices: This, of course, is not important in mail order selling because the printed advertising is, in effect, your store. Dorothy studied the sales letters, accompanying brochures, and, of course, the magazine ads inviting people to send for the literature.

Customer policies: Having bought a number of courses, Dorothy quickly learned how the companies handled sales and dealt with customers after the sale. She actually *took* the courses—studied them as a regular customer might—and wrote inquiries to the firm when she thought regular customers might.

"I learned many things about the correspondence course business that I never would have learned in any other manner," Dorothy reports. "Checking back in older magazines, I learned which companies had been around the longest, and this showed me which ones were the most successful."

She utilized the selling methods of the older firms, adapting the methods to her own needs, and she prepared her own course much the way one of the other companies might have done it.

Following proven success methods, her course was profitable right from the beginning. She is now selling several other home study courses in addition to the one that got her started, and she's had feelers from big-time firms seeking to buy her out. Her company has become a valuable property, and being a creative copycat is what made Dorothy a "self-made" millionaire.

YOU CAN DO IT IN NEARLY ANY FIELD

Because of their very nature, businesses cannot be secret operations, at least legitimate businesses can't. To be successful, they must constantly place their product or service and their methods before the public. And since they can't hide their success, it's easy to spot the winners you want to emulate.

It doesn't matter what money-making field you seek to enter; even writing books. In a cover story on "The Hot New Rich," *Time*

Magazine told of Robin Cook, who spent six months reading 100 best sellers to decide "what would capture the interest of the largest group of people."

His reading told him that a combination medical-mystery-thriller would do best for him. So he wrote *Coma*, which promptly made the best-seller lists itself, and was the featured selection of a major book club.

In effect, Robin Cook had done what the president of that hamburger chain suggested to the junior executive. He had gone out and dissected the best-selling "hamburgers" in his field.

PROFIT BY FOLLOWING THE LEADERS

A lot of people ask me why they should be creative copycats when they might become even richer by being the first to do something new in a given business field. I explain that the odds are a lot more in your favor when you follow a proven formula instead of trying to create one.

While a few SMMs have earned their fortunes being truly original, most did it the other way. An SMM in the latter category comments: "There is very little point in being the first to develop a unique product or service. The minute you do, others will be following close on your heels. *You* have gone to all the expense of research and development, and *they* benefit from all the trouble you've gone to."

This is why it usually pays to be a follower instead of a leader. "It's a perfectly honorable way of doing business," this SMM explains. "Nobody can patent a general business idea, and that's all we're talking about . . . adapting ideas to your own use and profiting from them." Thus, smart wealth-builders adapt other people's formulas throughout their money-making careers. Let's see how you can find formulas that:

1. Have built giant incomes for others working in the field you've chosen.
2. Can be adapted from one business field to another.
3. Can build your empire to million-dollar status and keep it there.

HOW TO ACCUMULATE
WEALTH-BUILDING FORMULAS

Much of this book deals with how to find the right business to match your high income goals, but for now let's assume you've decided on what type of business is best for you, and that you've reached the point where you need to know how to run it with methods already proven by SMMs working in that field. How do you latch on to these wealth-building methods? By going out and studying the hamburgers—in any legitimate way you can.

A Yugoslavian immigrant came to this country with only $20 in his pocket and the dream of starting an international pharmaceutical house. While a graduate chemistry student in California, Milan Panic invested $200 to get his business started.

He began by preparing chemicals for existing pharmaceutical firms to use in the preparation of their products. Mind you, selling chemicals to pharmaceutical houses was not his goal; it was his means. He couldn't afford to do drug research, but by dealing with companies that were doing the expensive research he learned a lot.

He was able to visit their laboratories, speak with their experts, and watch where the drug field was going. As profits began to mount from his sales, Panic was brought closer to his goal. Convincing friends and business associates to join in the investment, he was able to merge with an existing company in the health field for $10,000 down and a pile of convertible notes. This acquisition was followed by purchases of a string of companies in the pharmaceutical field.

Milan Panic's International Chemical and Nuclear Corporation became a multi-million-dollar entity within a matter of a few years, having nearly 5,000 employees on its payroll. Its number one "employee"—Milan Panic himself—had become a millionaire many times over.

FORMULA-FINDING THROUGH "INVOLVEMENT"

What Panic did to launch his empire was to become involved with existing businesses in his chosen field—the corporate "SMMs" of the pharmaceutical world. It wasn't their *chemical* formulas he sought; that sort of thing he could eventually develop on his own. What he did seek and obtain was a valuable insight into what directions he should pursue and what business policies he should follow. He learned these by seeing firsthand what the successful companies were doing.

In the last chapter we discussed learning a field by going to work for an existing company. But as Milan Panic demonstrated, there are other ways to become involved. Here are some of the ways *you* can learn an industry inside-out:

1. As Panic did, enter into a business relationship with existing companies. Start a small service or supply firm of your own. At this stage, profit is your secondary goal. Industry knowledge is the first.

2. Subscribe to trade publications and newsletters in the field. Look them up in the library by referring to *Business Publication Rates and Data*, published by Standard Rate and Data Service, Inc., and in the *Standard Periodical Directory*, published by Oxbridge Publishing Co., Inc. Trade publications tell you what's happening now in your industry and what's likely to happen in the future.

3. Attend seminars. One of America's fastest-growing industries is the commercial seminar, and they're given in nearly every business field. It can cost several hundred dollars to enroll in a one-to-three-day event, but you'll learn from the "biggies" in your field—giving you exposure to experts you probably wouldn't otherwise be able to meet at this stage of your career. Seminars are advertised in the trade periodicals, and when you subscribe to these publications, you can be sure your name will be put on mailing lists used by seminar sponsors to advertise their upcoming events.

4. Recruit from within the industry. Lacking the inside knowledge yourself, you can join up with someone else who has worked in your chosen field. If you're financially able, you can hire away such an expert (big corporations do this all the time, and many SMMs got their start doing the same thing). If you can't afford to meet a payroll yet, get an insider as a partner in your venture.

5. Enlist a close relative. Maybe you need to hold on to your present job until you are well established in your own business empire. So why not get your spouse, or a brother or sister, or even a potential future partner to take a job within the industry? Fred G. suggested that his wife do this several years ago when she was preparing to re-enter the work force. He had been thinking of going into the manufacture of hobby kits. There was a similar firm nearby, and his wife got a job there as a secretary. She learned a lot about how such companies are run, and she provided Fred with valuable information on suppliers, sales methods, trade publications, etc.

Let me stress again that none of this should involve the use of trade secrets. Finding out and using somebody else's trade secrets is immoral and illegal and won't get you very far because whatever profits you earn will probably have to be spent on defense attorneys. What we're speaking of here is gaining practical knowledge in a field, learning what the insiders do to build profits.

As an example, if you were to recruit somebody from a leading soft drink manufacturer to help you start your own cola business, you could copy their manufacturing and sales *methods*—but not the precise ingredients that go into their product.

Now let's move on to a second way that use of profit plans can make you rich.

ADAPT AN EXISTING FORMULA TO A DIFFERENT FIELD

Do you remember that in Chapter 2 I advised you to jot down, in your money-project notebook, unique business methods that intrigue you—whether or not they involve the kind of project you're thinking of? The reason for this is that a formula that works well in one field can often do just as well or even better in another.

How do you think King Gillette thought of the safety razor? Believe it or not, it started with the Crown Cork. The developer of the cork that was used for so many years inside the caps of soft-drink bottles—William Painter—was Gillette's inspiration

Knowing that Gillette was trying to dream up a fantastically profitable invention of his own, Painter pointed to the cork. He explained that its profit came from being a disposable item—

something the customer has to obtain over and over again.

Gillette began thinking about this—and while shaving one day, he got the idea for the safety razor with its throwaway blades. At that time, people used permanent blades that continually needed stropping to remain sharp, and occasionally they had to be taken to a cutler for professional sharpening.

Gillette envisioned a razor with blades that could be replaced inexpensively when they became dull. It would be something the customer would have to buy over and over again.

By adapting the Crown Cork theory to another field, King Gillette became rich.

ADAPTABLE FORMULAS ARE EVERYWHERE

The kind of adaptation Gillette did is being done to this day—and perhaps more than ever. A particular business method will prove itself in one field and then a clever entrepreneur comes along and uses the same thing in his field. Here are some examples:

- McDonald's is generally credited with establishing the fast food, limited menu restaurant. The efficiency comes from the limited menu. Employees learn to make a few things rapidly, cheaply, and well. This has been adapted by fast print shops which do one limited type of printing while you wait.

- Drive-in banks have led to drive-up photo kiosks in shopping centers, where you leave off your film to be developed and then pick it up in a day or two.

- Self-service laundries sparked the idea for self-service car washes where you insert a coin or two and clean your own car.

- The success of book clubs has led to record clubs and similar sales schemes in such varied fields as art, coins, and other collectors' items.

Thus, what you see done well in one industry can help you make a fortune in another industry. Keep your eye out for unusual business methods that:

- Make it easier or more convenient for customers to do business with you

- Increase profits while maintaining quality
- Provide customers with important cost savings

Emma L. was able to do this after becoming intrigued with her husband's constant patronage of auto supply stores. He was saving money by performing the routine service needed on his family's three cars, instead of taking them to the garage.

"It had been a hobby type of thing with him," Emma reports, "and I began searching for a way I could set up a business catering to hobby-oriented *women*." The result was a do-it-yourself store selling supplies for a wide variety of crafts, ranging from picture framing to sculpture, oil painting, drapery making, dressmaking, home decorating, and specialty cooking.

"The auto store wasn't the only business idea I borrowed from," Emma says. "I also took a leaf from the electronic kit companies and the home study courses in TV repair. Big areas in all my stores are devoted to kits and courses in the various crafts."

All her stores? Yes, the first venture led to the opening of many branches in other cities. Emma has become an SMM.

HOW TO PICK THE FORMULA THAT FITS YOU BEST

The formula that fits you best can usually be found right in front of your eyes. It just takes a little bit of training to learn how to recognize it. As I've noted, it generally is wise, when searching for a big money project, to stick to the field in which you've had the most experience.

Just as you can adapt existing formulas to a different field, you can make new use of a formula that already exists in your own field. Let me give you two examples:

- George Spitzer's field was distributing vitamins and diet foods to drug stores, but he didn't make really big money until he adapted a formula used by distributors of another type of product. Spitzer noted the success of home permanents, allowing women to do at home what formerly could only be accomplished in beauty salons. This gave him the idea for allowing men to obtain at home what formerly they could only get at the barber shop—instant shave cream lather. So he developed Rise shave cream, which for the first time provided lather at the push of a button atop a small can.

- Berry Gordy's field was music. He achieved a bit of success writing and producing records that were sold to record companies—but he didn't like the fact that he got such a small cut of the proceeds. So, borrowing some of the techniques of existing record companies, he invested $700 to start his own record company. Perhaps you've heard of Motown. It made this black entrepreneur a multi-millionaire.

Here's the way to pick the formula that fits you best:

1. Search first in your own field. Your experience will give you a head start in establishing your own business, and it will help you spot the trends and techniques that have achieved the most success for others.

2. As George Spitzer did, look for trends that can be adapted to new areas in your own field. He spotted a trend that enabled people to give themselves "professional" treatment at home. He borrowed from Toni Home Permanent to create Rise shave cream. If your field is accounting, you might borrow from the trend toward computerization and buy a relatively inexpensive minicomputer to allow you to provide computerized bookkeeping and payroll services for small businesses.

3. Berry Gordy looked to where the big profits were in his field. He found that recording companies made a lot more money than their individual producers, and his experience in the field enabled him to get started with a tiny investment.

4. If, after searching your own field, you are still attracted to some other type of enterprise, look for *adaptable* techniques. Many business formulas are universal. Being disposable and needing constant replacement is what built Crown Corks and, later, Gillette razor blades. Specializing in efficiently producing high volume in a limited line of products is what built McDonald's and all of its successful imitators in that and many other fields. Instant hambur-

gers led to instant printing, just as coin operated laundries brought on automatic car washes.

HOW SMALL CHANGE BRINGS BIGGER DOLLARS

William Rosenberg already had a successful business, in fact two of them, when he hit on the change that skyrocketed him to the really big time. He had opened a doughnut shop, and the success of the first outlet led him to open another.

Was the success of both stores merely a local phenomenon? Rosenberg had to find out, so he embarked on a cross country trip. He found that other people all over the country were achieving similar success. And he also found that nearly all of the stores were individually owned, purely local, businesses.

He thought of what a national chain with national promotion and advertising could do. Thus he began franchising his store, which has become the best known company in its field: Dunkin' Donuts.

What William Rosenberg did, in effect, was to make a small change in an existing industry. He gave nationwide identity to the doughnut shop, and it caught on like—well, like doughnuts.

You, too, can make a small change in an existing industry and get rich. Take Saul Steinberg as another example. With a small investment, he went into the computer leasing business—a field dominated by giants such as IBM.

But Steinberg's idea was to go IBM one better. The big companies were charging whopping premiums to customers who wanted the privilege of being able to cancel a lease before the contract expired. Steinberg figured, and correctly, that by offering non-cancellable leases with long-term contracts he could offer much lower rates.

He could and he did. His Leasco Data Processing Equipment Corporation is now one of the giants itself. It's made its founder a multi-multi-millionaire.

TWO CHANGES THAT CAN MAKE YOU RICH

Let's look again at what William Rosenberg and Saul Steinberg did. Two opposite things, actually. Rosenberg changed the retail doughnut industry by improving on what little mom and pop stores were doing. Steinberg changed the computer industry by improving on what the giants were doing. How can *you* do this sort of thing?

1. See what tiny business firms are succeeding at individually and build a large organization doing the same thing on a big scale, or

2. See what the established giants are doing and provide customers with a more economical alternative.

"Me, fight the big companies?" you ask. Certainly. Some of the big ones are so big they can't easily change. They dominate a field and think they can get whatever they demand of their customers. Then a little guy comes along, is a lot more flexible, and signs up one customer after another. He doesn't remain little for very long.

Take a look at any field, preferably *your* field, the one in which your work experience has been. See what the giants are doing, and especially what they're doing wrong. Right the wrong, starting on a small scale, and you should find that scale growing day by day. But one day, when *you* are a giant in the field, remember what got you started.

HOLD ON TO YOUR MILLION-DOLLAR STATUS

Being a creative copycat will serve you well throughout your business career—not only in getting ideas for your initial venture, but also in building it to million-dollar status and keeping it there. Successful entrepreneurs are constantly watching the competition and adapting many of its best techniques.

"I've gotten some of my best ideas watching what the others are doing," Henry T. reports. Henry became an SMM in the field of regional magazine publishing. "At first, my publications were written for *residents* of the areas they serve, and contained feature stories and picture spreads on interesting local people, activities, and places."

But then he found it more and more difficult to come up with material that was not already being adequately covered in the newspapers. "As the local papers became larger and more successful, they had to resort to feature-type items to fill their pages.

Readership of my magazines began to drop."

While traveling in another area of the country, Henry naturally stopped by at a magazine stand to see how regional publications were doing there. "And I found they catered more to tourists and visitors than to full-time residents. They were, in effect, guides to the area, issued on a monthly basis, and they sold most of their advertising to restaurants, tourist attractions, and other places catering to visitors.

It was easy for Henry to make the slight change in the format of his publications. As a result, they are now doing better than ever.

Millionaire restaurateur Winston Schuler enhanced his financial standing by regularly visiting other eating establishments across the land, obtaining many good ideas that way. His field trips away from his establishment in Michigan were planned so he could evaluate the other restaurants through the eyes of a patron instead of a professional in the field. This has helped make him aware of what his own customers might like.

PROFIT FROM THE SUCCESS OF YOUR COMPETITORS

Whenever Frank N., the owner of a chain of book stores, hears of unusual promotions conducted by other book stores, and whenever he hears of the outstanding success of a particular establishment, he sends a staff member out to investigate.

"I've never stopped learning from what the others are doing," Frank says. "In fact, the way I operate is to let them try out the new schemes and promotional techniques. Some of these methods succeed, others fail. I pick up the ones that are obviously successful. What works for others will almost always work for me."

Thus, success formulas originated by others can help you in many ways. Here are just some:

- You keep up-to-date with the latest profit techniques.
- You learn new ways to deal with business problems that are common throughout your industry.
- Unusual methods of attracting and keeping customers come to your attention.
- You avoid much of the trouble and expense of the trial-

and-error technique, because your competitors do it for you.

EXAMINE THESE MILLIONAIRE SECRETS

In the course of this chapter you've read about a number of specialized techniques that have made people rich. These are what I call "millionaire secrets," and they bring success regardless of the field in which they are applied.

Examine this list of millionaire secrets carefully. One or more of them can be the secret to your future success. I suggest writing them down in your money-project notebook to remind you to be constantly on the lookout for means of applying these powerful self-enrichment methods.

Here's the list:

- Dissect the best-selling products or services in your field. Examine them bit by bit not only to learn how you can offer the same thing, but improve upon it. Don't go in for fancy research, just look at what the competition is doing.

- Don't aim at being the first to try something. Let the others go through the trial-and-error process for you. Profit from their successes as well as their errors.

- Realize that nobody can patent a general business idea or keep a successful idea secret for very long. This is why their success can breed your success.

- Get inside information legitimately by hiring or going into partnership with professionals in the field, and by attending seminars and studying trade publications. Also consider entering into a business relationship with existing firms to learn more about how they operate.

- Find a formula that works well in one field and adapt the same idea to another field. This can also be done within two different areas of the same field.

- Lure customers away from the giant firms by offering incentives that the big firms refuse to make available.

- Find what a lot of small companies are doing well individually and build a big operation doing the same thing on a nationwide scale.

- Keep on top, once you are established, by continuing to watch the competition and adapting its tried and proven techniques.

These are truly potent methods for achieving vast wealth. You've seen them applied in the examples given throughout this chapter. Any one of them can make you a multi-millionaire.

6

Build a Bonanza by Updating the Outdated

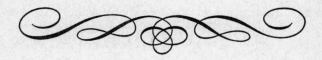

Find a business field where the methods have not quite kept up with the times and you've got yourself a million-dollar opportunity. By introducing modern techniques, you can reap profits that are being overlooked by your long-established competitors. This chapter tells how to do it.

WHERE OTHERS FAIL, YOU HAVE TO WIN

A lot of businessmen who have made good money for years see no reason for changing their methods. Then a smart competitor steps in, creates some small changes to update the outdated, and he makes a mint.

Opportunities to use this strategy exist everywhere, have always existed, and always will exist. Why is that? Because in this constantly changing world, everything, including money-making methods, has its day—and its twilight. It is surprising how many companies, big and small, fail to recognize the twilight periods of their own long-established methods.

Some historical examples:

99

- When electric refrigerators came in, most ice-making companies were forced out of business. But *some* ice-makers are still making big money today by selling cubes and blocks through roadside vending machines.
- The printing industry was revolutionized by the arrival of offset reproduction, using photographic techniques instead of setting metal type. Printers who stuck to hand typesetting found themselves losing out to newcomers using the cheaper and more efficient offset process.
- Many portrait photographic studios were forced to close when an increasing number of families began to satisfy their own photographic needs with easy-to-use cameras. But the *smart* commercial photographers continue to flourish by adapting their methods and taking on new kinds of photographic work.

"WHY DON'T THEY . . .?" CAN LEAD TO A FORTUNE

How many times have you asked yourself, "Why don't they . . ." and then concluded the sentence with some suggestion for improving a product or service? I'm sure this has happened many times, and you've probably had some good ideas on how "they" could do it. Well, the purpose of this chapter is to convert the "they" to *you*. Since they are not doing it, you can . . . and earn a fortune.

START SMALL, GROW BIG

You don't have to buck the industrial giants in order to profit from updating the outdated. You can get started on a very small scale. Here is a perfect case in point.

Ian H., who worked as a TV repairman, purchased a digital wristwatch in a local department store, only to have it malfunction several months after the guarantee ran out. He took it to a local jeweler, but he said that he wasn't equipped to repair it; his training had been in wind-up watches. He went back to the discount house where he bought the watch—but they told him to send it to the manufacturer for service.

Now, of course, having to mail a watch and wait weeks and

perhaps months for it to be returned can be a great inconvenience. But for Ian it provided a great opportunity. He checked around and found that *most* jewelers were not repairing electronic watches, although they usually did arrange to obtain factory replacements for watches that they had originally sold. However, most electronic watches are sold in discount stores, which don't want to see them again. So Ian updated the outdated. He became an "electronic jeweler," meaning he started an electronic watch repair service.

"Actually, I don't repair most watches," Ian is quick to explain. "Their 'works' are produced so inexpensively that it's generally cheaper merely to replace the innards, although before doing this I check for corrosion or obvious breaks in the printed circuit."

Ian's company serves jewelers in a tri-state area, making twice-weekly pickups and deliveries. The jewelers are happy because they can now arrange for electronic watch repairs without much bother, and, at the same time, perhaps establish lasting business relationships with potential new customers. The customers are happy because they can get service within three or four days. And Ian is happy because his business has reached million-dollar status.

SEE WHAT THE INSIDERS DON'T SEE

It's an unfortunate fact of business life (but fortunate for you) that many long-established veterans in a given business field don't spot the opportunities that are virtually knocking at their doors. They try to improve their products or services, true, but only by established methods. They "know" what can and what can't be done, and they never flirt with the impossible.

Then an outsider comes along who doesn't know enough about a certain business to realize what is and what is not impossible. And, of course, he achieves what the oldtimers had ruled out long before.

Take paint rollers as an example. Nothing really new there— they had been invented and patented in the 1800's. But they'd never been very practical. Rollers manufactured out of carpeting material worked well with water-based paints, but not at all with oil-based products.

Along came Vern Touchett, an industry outsider who thought up the idea of using lamb's wool as the material. He tried it—it worked just fine with oil-based paints—and thus was born the E Z Paintr Corporation. He convinced major retailers to handle the new product, and homeowners quickly took to it as well.

Although Touchett became an insider, he retained the outsider's instincts, and it's well that he did, because, when latex-based paints came on the market, his lamb's wool rollers became useless—just as carpeting had years before with the oil paints.

But Touchett (and his brothers who had joined him in business) knew that if they didn't come up with the answer, someone else would, so they experimented. And their answer was synthetic fibers.

This innovation, too, was successful, and the company has since expanded into other areas of the decorating products field.

FRESH EYES REJUVENATE OLD PRODUCTS

Does it seem possible that the giants in the painting field had never thought of using lamb's wool on paint rollers? After all, lambs have been around for almost as long as animals have trod the earth. Paint rollers had been around for a century by the time Vern Touchett entered the business. But no insider had ever thought of combining those two old commodities—wool and paint rollers.

As you progress through this chapter you'll learn this:

Many businesses—and even entire industries—are enmeshed in their own ruts. Millions can be made with simple innovations that lie right before your eyes.

And, many times, all it takes is a slight new twist to set you up for a lifetime of superabundant wealth.

HOW TO CREATE "NEW TWIST" OPPORTUNITIES

There are scores of business fields just begging for a new twist. They're ripe for the profiteer who learns how to spot them and apply the twist that can generate bigger profits than the old-timers ever thought possible.

Surprisingly, the easiest way to do this is to find the "twist" first and *then* find the business that it fits. This gives you the solution practically before you start. It's a lot like the way many mystery writers put together their "whodunit" novels; with the solution well in mind when they start, it's a lot easier to assemble the clues that are to come earlier in the book.

So here's how to create your own "new twist" business opportunity:

1. Pick a new product, service, or trend that has been proven successful in one or more business fields.

2. Apply that innovation to an appropriate business field where it has not been generally used before.

As I say, finding the solution first and the problem second makes things a lot easier than if you were to do it the more "logical" way.

The experiences of some of the millionaires you've already met in this book will prove my point:

- Before he ever dreamed of starting a world-wide fast-food chain, Ray Kroc discovered the "solution"—the system developed by the McDonald Brothers in California. *Then* he set out to apply it across the nation and around the world.

- Truck driver Jim Walter wasn't thinking of going into the home-building business when he spotted an ad for a shell-house. But it seemed like such a perfect solution to meeting the need for low-cost housing that he began using it as a fortune-building method. It made him rich.

- It wasn't until someone tried to buy their slingshot that Richard Knerr and Spud Melin thought of manufacturing such products. The "solution" they started with was the public's craving for novelty items, and, as you've read, their slingshots led to Hula Hoops and Frisbees and other million-dollar money-makers.

- King Gillette saw the vast amount of money being made by producing items that become useless and must be replaced soon after they're bought. He spotted the potential money-maker in bottle caps—and then adapted the idea to a new field—razor blades.

- George Spitzer noticed that good money was being made by such firms as Toni Home Permanents that allow people to give themselves professional treatment at home. If it worked with hairdos, why not with full-lather shave creams? Until that point, no one had thought of providing that item for home use.

As you can see, the solution you find can be applied in the same business field where you found it, or it can be applied to an entirely different type of business.

PICK A TWIST RIGHT DOWN YOUR ALLEY

It has been mentioned several times in this book that, everything else being equal, you should try to stick to a field with which you are already familiar. And when it comes to "new twist" opportunities, this applies more than ever. Why? Because that's the easiest place for you to find new trends that are adaptable to other business ideas.

Here are some examples to guide you:

- If you work with computers, try to think of a field in which they have not been extensively used.
- Let's say you're a bus driver. Buses have been around for many years, but there are many untapped uses for them.
- Perhaps you're an aviation engineer, working with metals that are strong but light. Find a different field where these same metals can be used.

"Easier said than done!" you complain. Perhaps; and then again, perhaps not. You see, in each of these three examples, *it has been done*. Learning how, and by whom, should help you develop your own new twist.

Computers: John Mallon had a working familiarity with both computers and crime. He had seen both in operation in his work as a newspaper reporter. Most detective agencies, in the late 1960's and early 1970's, were still using cloak and dagger techniques. Why not use computers and other electronic marvels to help track down criminals for pay? Thus was born IBI Security Systems, Inc., with an initial investment of $3,000. Within three years, it was in the multi-million-dollar category.

Buses: Frank T. was a bus driver for a suburban transport firm. When the vehicle he had driven for many years was about to be retired because of high mileage, he realized that somebody would get a good buy. Its diesel engine and other mechanical parts were still in excellent working order; not for heavy duty maybe, but still functioning well. Who got the good buy? *He* did. He bought it from his employer and then set about converting it into a motor home for his family's travels. Then he began buying other used buses and converting them as well, selling them at good profit to other people who recognized their value.

Aviation metals: Howard Head knew how aviation had advanced when planes began to be made out of metal rather than doped fabric. The light and durable materials developed by the aviation industry should be useful in other fields as well, right? Right. A skiing enthusiast, Head went to the drawing board and came up with a metal ski that was an improvement over the traditional hickories. Hundreds of thousands of them have been sold.

HOW TO PICK A MILLION-DOLLAR INNOVATION

In recent years, you've seen the new twist formula in action many times. Think of the TV game craze. Packaged games such as Monopoly and darts had been around for years. So had TV sets. Then smart innovators combined the two and cleaned up financially.

Computers were nothing new, and neither was the do-it-yourself trend. Then a company in the west began selling build-it-yourself computer kits to home hobbyists, and a new industry was launched.

Books have been around ever since Gutenberg printed his first Bible. Cassette tape recorders have been on the scene since the 1960's. Then along came a company recording books on tape and renting the tapes to people who could benefit from hearing books read to them in their spare moments—while driving a car or shaving, etc. A new source of profits was tapped.

You can create your own similar innovation. Just look around you.

- On your job you are familiar with procedures that, with a little imagination, can be applied to other fields.
- Feature reports in the press, and on radio and TV, constantly tell of interesting products and services. Think of how some of these can be used in new ways.

- The products you use every day in your home or for your
  hobby can be helpful in other areas as well.

It doesn't matter how routine your job or hobbies may appear
to be. In pursuing them, you have come across procedures and
products that are adaptable to new, as yet unthought-of, profit-
making procedures.

FROM $170 PER WEEK TO MILLIONAIRE STATUS

Jan L. was earning $170 per week as a secretary to an insur-
ance broker. One day, while reading a secretarial magazine, she
came across an article telling of automatic typewriters with
"memories." Once a page is typed on these machines, its text is
stored in an electronic memory that will have the machine retype it
at the push of a button. And the result can be personalized with
typed-in insertions that make it appear to be a letter prepared
individually for the recipient.

The article explained that many large companies were using
automatically typed letters to speed correspondence with their customers. In many such cases, these letters were more effective than
the older "form letters" that had long been in use.

Jan thought that if these letters are so effective in holding on to
customers, they should be just as valuable in collecting from customers. She knew that most business firms have difficulty in collecting past-due accounts. In such cases, they (1) send out form
collection letters, (2) spend a lot of time writing personal letters, or
(3) turn the matter over to collection agencies.

How about low-cost, personalized, collection letters? Standard wording could be used throughout most of the letter, along
with the debtor's name and a personal plea to pay up inserted
manually where appropriate. Jan contacted several companies and
found them to be interested in the idea. So she rented an automatic
typewriter and set up shop.

Her list of clients grew rapidly, and before long Jan had
purchased one, and then two, and then several machines. She now
has a staff of salesmen offering her firm's services to companies in
several states. Business volume has reached the multi-million-
dollar level, and the company has several branch offices in key
cities.

HOW TO GET IN CHEAP AND COME OUT RICH

Across the United States—and throughout the free world, for that matter—are thousands of little businesses based on a unique or innovative idea. These little firms may or may not be making much money for their owners, but they have a potential for great development, a potential that the owner has not exploited.

Along comes someone with an SMM mentality, he or she obtains the rights to the business (sometimes without having to put up any money) and the unique idea takes off like a skyrocket.

Ray Kroc discovered such an opportunity in the California hamburger establishment he visited. He spotted the vast potential and obtained the rights to develop McDonald's for a small royalty, agreeing to pay one-half of one percent of the proceeds. Later, after McDonald's became a giant empire, he bought out the brothers for $2.7-million.

Jim Walter's giant construction empire was based on a discovery he made while looking for a home for himself—shell houses, as advertised by a small local builder. Jim Walter gave the concept the development it so badly needed.

And then there's someone whom you have not met so far in this book—Charles Doolin. He had been looking for a packaged snack product to produce, and it was while having lunch in a small restaurant one day that he spotted a small package of corn chips. They were just what he was looking for. Doolin looked up the "manufacturer," a Mexican national who was interested in returning to his homeland. For $100 he sold Doolin his corn-chip producing machinery and the recipe. Doolin took it from there. Perhaps you've enjoyed the product he developed—Fritos. And the company now also produces dozens of other snack items.

THREE WAYS TO OBTAIN BUSINESS RIGHTS

In the above three examples, you've seen in action the three ways *you* can obtain the rights to an underdeveloped business idea without having to put up much cash. Here they are:

Royalty basis: As Ray Kroc did, you may be able to work out a royalty or commission arrangement with the owner. The one-half of one percent gave Kroc unlimited franchise rights to the McDonald's restaurant idea. After profits have mounted, you can, as Kroc did, afford to buy out the originators.

Partnership basis: Like Jim Walter, you can go into partnership with the originator of the idea. *He* has the technical knowhow, *you* provide the needed development and expansion.

Purchase basis: Often, the originator may not recognize, or be interested in pursuing, the potential of his idea. And thus it can probably be obtained cheaply. Such was the case when Charles Doolin bought the rights to what became Fritos. (Incidentally, even the $100 he paid was not all his own money. He employed OPM by borrowing one-fourth of that amount.)

As you have seen, latching on to an innovative idea originated by others is one route SMMs have taken to launch their empires. Now let's move on to the second method.

UTILIZE YOUR OWN ASSETS

You may already have in your own possession something that can become the basis of a new twist opportunity, revolutionizing an industry and making a fortune for you. What you have may not be extremely valuable in the way you have used it up to now, but, applied in a new field, it could be the spark that puts your business genius in high gear.

What might you have now that could lead to a new twist in the world of business? It could be any of the following:

- Specialized knowledge
- Physical possessions
- Ownership of an existing business

Perhaps all you need to do is utilize one of these assets in a *new direction*—something neither you nor many other people have thought of previously. Let's see how it's done with each of these asset categories.

CASH IN ON SPECIALIZED KNOWLEDGE

Take hobbies as an example. Most people, when thinking of a way to build a business based on their hobbies, take the standard route. Many succeed, but some of the biggest successes have been achieved by those who have used their hobby-related knowledge to add a new twist to a business in an entirely different field.

Cy P. was involved in electronics, having started with kit-building and grown into the design and construction of his own electronic circuits. The standard route for a person such as Cy to take might have been TV repair or some other kind of electronic maintenance.

But Cy didn't take that route. Fascinated by the computerized marvels at Disneyland and Walt Disney World, he set out to design and build computerized entertainment features for amusement parks. His talking mannequins, light spectaculars, and multi-media presentations are now seen in many parts of the United States. His firm supplies and maintains the equipment running these shows, and Cy is a self-made millionaire.

"Yes, but he must be a genius," you say. Perhaps. What he did, though, took no more ability than programming computers for more routine functions such as record-keeping. He just gave it a different twist. He used electronics in a fairly new field.

You can do the same with your hobby-related knowledge. If your hobby is, say, woodworking, don't limit your business possibilities to cabinetmaking. You might do as Doug M. did and start a firm that does custom work on yacht interiors. Most of today's boats are not only plastic on the outside, they are plastic on the inside as well. Doug deals with well-to-do yachtsmen, providing them with the warm-looking wood interiors they crave and which are missing in today's production-line craft. His outfit has branches in several of the major yachting areas of the United States.

MAKE USE OF YOUR PHYSICAL POSSESSIONS

Just as specialized knowledge can launch your new twist business opportunity, special possessions such as work-producing equipment can do the same. Some examples:

- A midwesterner who owned sophisticated camera equipment sought to make money in photography. He bypassed the usual commercial photography route, and instead he opened a processing laboratory for serious amateur photographers. He knew that the standard mail-order labs were not able to meet the individual needs of first-rate photographers by using their automated equipment. His custom work demands top dollar, and it draws customers throughout the country.

- A southern widow who was left with an empty factory building when her husband died (his business having dissolved during his long illness) searched for tenants for the structure, but could find none. What do you do with a factory building that nobody wants? You might, as she did, convert it into a unique shopping mall—with booths, stalls, and small stores for hundreds of rent-paying merchants. The bazaar-type atmosphere was an immediate hit with shoppers and the originator of the idea sold the building several years later for $3½ million.

GIVE YOUR EXISTING BUSINESS A NEW TWIST

I've found that many readers of my books and articles are people who have tried business before without achieving the success they sought. They may still be in business, part or full time, but are not happy with the results.

When these people seek my professional counseling, I often suggest they re-examine their business assets. Obviously, something has not been done correctly. It could be, as I told Frank and Marilyn V., that they have the right tools but are using them on the wrong job.

This couple had launched a home-based mail-order business, selling recordings they had made of the orchestra and chorus at a nearby college.

"We've received orders, true," Marilyn explained, "but not nearly enough to pay for our magazine advertising."

I asked her why they had chosen to sell the discs through the mail. "Because it seemed like an easy way to sell," she replied. "We can't really peddle these things door to door."

"Mail order can be an easy way to sell, provided you have the right type of product," I explained, "but your type of product is best sold another way, and it can be done at far less expense." They were obviously interested in what I had to say, so I continued.

"Your recordings sell for $6.98, and you tell me they cost you $2.00 each—for the master recording and the pressings you sell. That leaves you a $5.00 margin. Let's say your selling expense amounted to $2.00. That would leave $3.00 for overhead and profit. How does that sound to you?"

"Wonderful!" they said in unison.

"O.K., think of this. Who has the most interest in your recordings? Students at the college and their parents, right? And there are 5,000 students at the school." They nodded.

"The solution is to have a student organization sell the recordings on campus as a fund-raising effort. Give them a $2.00 cut. You'll find they'll be happy to do it."

"But," Frank interjected, "we probably could only sell a thousand or two records that way. Hardly enough for a going business."

"More than enough," I responded, "when you take into account the hundreds of colleges and millions of students in the United States. You can use your recording equipment to make LP's at many schools—and sell the discs right back to the same schools, through student fund-raising campaigns."

Frank and Marilyn took my advice, and their company soon began to show a profit. They've dealt with more than a dozen schools so far and they are now in a major expansion phase. I predict that within a few years—if they keep it up and use growth techniques similar to those outlined in this book—they will become self-made millionaires.

NEW USE FOR EXISTING TOOLS

Frank and Marilyn did not change their basic business—recordings of student musical groups—they changed their selling method. They gave their business a new twist. Too many business people keep on plugging in the same old way and wonder why success doesn't come.

Laurens Hammond achieved success of sorts in many ventures, ranging from the manufacture of clocks to developing three-dimensional movies and phonograph turntables. But each time circumstances and competition kept him from reaching the golden apple.

Each of his products—the clocks, the movie equipment, and the turntables—had used a special synchronous electric motor he developed.

Then one day he decided to give a new twist both to his business and to an item that had been around for hundreds of years. He worked out a way to use that synchronous motor to power an electric organ— the first of its kind. I don't have to tell you what happened to the Hammond Organ Company. And I don't have to tell you that its founder became a multi-millionaire.

The point of all this? Simply that you may already have the assets with which your own million-dollar empire can be launched. Perhaps all you need is examination of what you have from a different perspective—a new twist, if you will.

FIND BARGAIN OPPORTUNITIES

So far we've discussed two of the ways SMMs take the new twist route in building their fortunes. The third and final method involves uncovering bargain opportunities in areas other people have overlooked. This kind of SMM sees "gold in them thar hills" when other people merely see a lot of seemingly useless land. So the entrepreneur moves in, buys what he seeks at bargain-basement prices, and comes out greatly enriched.

How do you find gold in them thar hills? Here's what you do:

Devise a new and profitable use for something that nobody else wants.

Those are 12 powerful words, when put together in the manner you see above. Those 12 words describe a method that has made hundreds of men and women fabulously rich. Why is this method so effective? For these reasons:

(1) A commodity that nobody wants can be purchased at rock-bottom prices.

(2) Devising a new use for that commodity gives it a greatly heightened value.

(3) The entrepreneur who buys and sells such commodities can achieve profit markups of fantastic percentages.

The method involves giving a new twist to an old item. What type of old item? Here's what some SMMs have done:

- Reprinted classics long out of copyright (thereby avoiding any royalty payments) and given them expensive-looking covers so they can sell for ten or more times the production costs.

- Imported thousands of old school clocks and sold them domestically on the antique market.

- Purchased what seemed to others to be next-to-worthless land—and then gave it the right kind of development that made buyers eager to pay top-dollar for it.

- Renewed the usefulness of decrepit-appearing but structurally sound old buildings, enhancing their value tremendously.

- Purchased the stock of failing retail outlets for much less than wholesale cost, selling it for close to retail value.

- Bought up factory over-production items, selling them with pinpoint advertising methods geared to reaching the people who can best use the items.

These are just a few of the ways people have become rich by devising new and profitable uses for commodities nobody else wanted.

A New Twist Expert

Earlier in this book, you met Peter Kanavos, who used ingenious methods to raise money for the chain of taverns that got his multi-million dollar empire started. Later, he moved into real estate.

His specialty? He concentrated on acquiring raw or lackluster properties at bargain prices. His goal? Turning them into big income-producers by using development and promotion. He has built shopping centers in swamps, and industrial parks in barren countryside.

Peter Kanavos became a new twist expert in land. The opportunities for doing the same thing—not only in land, but also in many other types of commodities—are as great today as ever.

HOW TO TIME YOUR MOVE FOR MAXIMUM PROFIT

In some cases, it's not what you do that counts as much as *when* you do it. Timing can play an important role when you seek to make a financial killing.

Samuel Goldwyn held off releasing his movies to TV for many years. Other producers led the way, quick to offer their productions to the television networks. Goldwyn sat on his reels and waited.

Why? Because he knew that these other producers, so anxious to gain a new market for their films, would *build a bigger market for him*. They created the public appetite for movies on TV. Prices paid by the networks rose and rose. Finally, Sam Goldwyn's productions were made available. And he got much more for them than if he had jumped on the bandwagon when most of his colleagues had started to.

Joseph Resnick made millions in TV, but on the other side of the tube. His money came from homes that needed antennas. As a TV repairman, he often struggled to install rooftop antennas, which, in the early days, came disassembled and were awkward to handle. Why couldn't they be made somewhat like umbrellas—opening up instantly? To do so would cut installation time and save a lot of money for homeowners as well as installers. Resnick had the right idea at the right time. He formed the Channel Master company, and it has become one of the leading firms in the electronics equipment field.

Some might say that Joe Resnick was lucky—thinking of a needed item at the right time. But who's to say for sure that he hadn't been searching for an important need to fill? His umbrella-like antenna was the right idea for that time.

There are thousands of "right" items (and services) needed today. Finding one of these needs and filling it is one way of timing your business move for maximum profit. The other is doing as Samuel Goldwyn did and watch the market develop—thereby being ready with a good product to sell when the market hits its peak.

Thus, you can benefit from precise timing in either of two ways:

(1) Offer a product or service that is needed today, and that is not being adequately provided by others.

(2) Pick a market that is just beginning to grow, let others spend their money creating consumer demand, and then move in to meet the requirements of a ready-made market.

EXAMINE THE NEW TWIST SPECTACULARS

Many different money-making methods are outlined in this book along with the experiences of numerous self-made millionaires. Some achieved their wealth in old established fields, others in emerging specialties. But nearly all employed at least a few "new twists" to help speed their way to the top. Watch for these twists as you continue reading.

Some to look for:

• Developing mass production techniques for an item that has been tediously produced by slow labor

• Locating a business where others have not dreamed of, and creating an entirely new market

• Taking one element of a successful business and building a worldwide empire based on that one element

• Taking a simple work skill learned on the job and converting it into a specialty for which thousands of people pay hundreds of dollars each

You won't have to wait long to learn how these twists were executed. They're all included in the next chapter.

7

How to Activate Your Million-Dollar Program

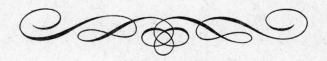

There's only one major difference between the average working person and the one who becomes a self-made millionaire. Learn that difference, do something about it, and you can close the gap—leaping from one category to the other.

What is the difference?

It's not hard work. Lots of people work hard, holding down two or three jobs, without getting rich.

It's not education. Look at all the college graduates struggling to make ends meet, and then compare their plight with the school "failures" and dropouts who have amassed fabulous fortunes.

It's not ideas. There's no shortage of workable, wealth-building ideas. We all get them. For instance, we all see things that need improving and know how we would do it "if given the chance."

And it's not lack of capital. Most of the wealthy people you're meeting in this book started with little or no cash. In fact, one you'll read about in this chapter began with *minus* ten thousand dollars!

So if it's not hard work, education, ideas, or capital, what *is* it that spells the difference between the low-paid employee and the

guy who in a few short years has built himself a life of absolute
luxury?

In a word, it's *action*. Not just dreaming up the Big Idea, but
putting it in motion. Most people sit on their ideas. Then somebody else who knows how simple it is to put a wealth-building
program in motion gets the same idea and makes a mint.

HOW TO MAKE YOUR FORTUNE SELF-PROPELLED

Your own money-making idea—perhaps one you obtain from
reading this book—can propel you as high as you want to go on the
financial ladder. You're about to learn how to:

1. Make the first vital move.
2. Make other moves that assure you of continued success.
3. Mushroom your program into an explosion of profits.

Be certain of one fact. Anyone with a good money-making idea
can take these three steps and move with absolute confidence toward his or her multi-million dollar goal.

Let me tell you about a man who started with nothing but a
good idea. He had no money—not even a college or high school
education. And his name has become one of the best known of all
American multi-millionaires. You see it wherever you go. The
name is Howard Johnson.

"If I was at all bright," says Howard Johnson, "it was the fact
that I realized that I had an idea that worked. And I followed it and
kept following it."

He got that idea when he was a teenager, and he nurtured it in
his mind until the time when he was old enough to strike out on his
own. While he was growing up, most restaurants were located
inside towns and cities. The main highways were mostly barren
except for service stations. And Howard Johnson figured that he
could draw double the patronage by building on the outskirts of
towns and cities. This way, he'd get the highway trade as well as
that of the townspeople.

MAKE THE FIRST VITAL MOVE

So did Howard Johnson immediately proceed to open a string
of orange-roofed restaurants? No more than you will proceed to fire

all your guns with one big blast. He couldn't have done it any more than you can do it. He took one step at a time.

And that first vital move was to open a store—a very small store—in Wollaston, Massachusetts. Actually, it was a tobacco shop that also held the local newspaper delivery franchise. He bought it with no money, putting himself into debt for $10,000.

Mr. Johnson recognized a significant thing. He couldn't live off the profits from selling tobacco, and the newspaper franchise could be taken away from him, leaving him with very little. So he developed a product nobody could take away from him—his own homemade ice cream. Other foodstuffs were added, and the little store became his first "restaurant."

It's important to note that for many years Howard Johnson had been nurturing that one Big Idea—highway restaurants—just as your Big Idea may be running through your own head right now. But if Howard Johnson hadn't made his first vital move, the move into a tiny store to perfect his program, today it might just be an idea that long ago was taken over by others.

MAKE OTHER MOVES
THAT ASSURE YOU OF CONTINUED SUCCESS

Knowing that his customers loved his ice cream, did Mr. Johnson then build up a string of restaurants? Hardly. He did what I want you to do, so you can be fully confident your idea will work. He tested it.

First he sold the ice cream to other stores. It passed the first major test when sales reached $200,000. That gave him the confidence to open a restaurant in a nearby town. In turn, the outstanding success of that outlet led to another, and another, and another.

There's a vital lesson to be learned here, and it's this:

You can guarantee your success, instead of gambling it, by testing each major move before you make it.

Your idea may not involve restaurants; it could be in real estate, or publishing, or mail order, or in a new product. Whatever it is, there are powerful ways of testing it so that you make all the right moves. You'll learn these methods in the next chapter, but I want you to know right now what a positive force testing can be in amassing your own million-dollar fortune.

MUSHROOM YOUR PROGRAM
INTO AN EXPLOSION OF PROFITS

If Howard Johnson had confined himself to selling ice cream—or even to operating his own restaurants—he'd be a rich man today, but not nearly as rich as he is. With the initial success of the ice cream and the first few restaurants, he had something else pulling for him—his *name*.

At that point, he still could not afford to open a big nationwide string of restaurants. So he franchised them, selling people the right to build orange-roofed eateries with the Howard Johnson name out front.

As you'll see in Chapter 12, franchising can be one of the most potent forces for converting a good idea into a fortune. Howard Johnson certainly found it so.

But he didn't stop there. His name is now on motels, on take-home candy products that you can purchase in his restaurants, and on foods you buy in the supermarket.

As your own wealth-building program develops, you'll discover this fact:

One venture can breed many others, and pyramid your profits beyond your original expectations.

You start with one Big Idea. But, just like the root of your family tree, that idea gives birth to offspring projects that can make you the patriarch of your own financial empire.

How *You* Can Do It

Making your fortune self-propelled, flowing from one profit-success to another, is accomplished by taking these steps:

1. Test and develop your idea. You won't be thoroughly convinced of its effectiveness until you try it out. Do so on a small scale, perfecting your techniques and spotting the special opportunities that only become evident after you've actually begun doing business.

2. Learn the business thoroughly. And there's no better way to do it than by becoming personally involved in all phases of the operation. It's more valuable to you than the best

degree from the nation's biggest business school. Realize you can make big profits while you learn. Two years after he started distributing ice cream, Howard Johnson took in $200,000.

3. As you learn, grow. Your education will continue as long as you own your empire, but your business will be expanding all the time. Each move prepares you for the next big step, which is what I mean by being self-propelled. Explore franchising, stock sales, acquisitions, and all of the other big money techniques outlined in Chapter 12.

CONVERT SETBACKS INTO OPPORTUNITIES

I can hear you saying it now. "I'm sure to make mistakes, and world or national conditions could throw my plans out of kilter." Yes, of course you'll make some mistakes. But that's what testing is for—to help you minimize your bloopers and maximize your triumphs. You literally test your way to success!

As for conditions over which you have no control, the alert fortune-builder discovers ways to turn them to his advantage. During the Second World War, Howard Johnson had to board up 90 percent of his restaurants. Gasoline rationing kept most people off the highways.

This could have spelled disaster for Howard Johnson's enterprise, but it didn't. The rationing of such commodities as cream and sugar to commercial firms was based on pre-war usage by those companies. This gave Mr. Johnson enough raw materials to continue making ice cream, even though he couldn't retail most of it himself. Instead, he sold it to inner city stores that managed to stay open. And he converted his food *serving* talents to meeting the needs of the military—in cafeterias, food preparation courses, and the like.

Disaster? Not at all. His dollar volume was bigger than before the war.

SIMPLE STEPS THAT FIRE UP YOUR MONEY MACHINE

An outsider who takes a look at a self-made millionaire's vast money-making organization can sometimes be awed at how complex it seems. "I could never do anything like that," says the outsider. "It's far too complicated."

What the outsider fails to realize is that the organization was assembled one step at a time. In fact, usually one *simple* step at a time.

Everyone who goes to work for the huge H&R Block tax preparation organization is given written instructions on how to do his or her job. And do you know the credo that heads the list of instructions? This is it:

Success is built one client at a time.

The Block organization was started by two brothers in Kansas City who rented desk space in an office for $25 a month. *Simple Step Number One.*

One brother used the desk to perform the services while the other went out soliciting clients. *Simple Step Number Two.*

At first they performed a variety of administrative services for business firms, doing tax preparation as a free added bonus. But they found that the tax work was the most sought after, so they began concentrating on that. *Simple Step Number Three.*

With the popularity of their service, the brothers expanded to other cities, often hiring temporary help during the tax season. *Simple Step Number Four.*

From there, the business mushroomed throughout the United States and other nations. Annual revenues exceeded $120 million.

But the important thing to remember is that their success was built one client at a time, just as their business was built one step at a time. You see, they didn't start out with the idea of running a $120 million business empire. Such thoughts may or may not have drifted through their heads, but their actual moves were taken simply and logically. They met an important need, and their enterprise was propelled into the multi-million dollar category.

And notice the fact that when experience showed them that *one* of their many business services—income tax preparation—was outperforming all the others, they began concentrating on that. Put another way, *they spotted a special opportunity that only became evident after they'd actually begun doing business.*

That's why *you* should begin as soon as possible to take the first simple steps to fire up *your* money machine. It has been proven time and again:

As profitable as your original idea may be, it can open up vast new potentials for wealth that you never dreamed of.

And unless you get started, unless you begin putting your program in motion, those opportunities will never open up to you.

THREE STEPS TO A MILLION DOLLARS

You read, a few pages back, of the three steps to take for making your fortune self-propelled: (1) Test and develop your idea; (2) Learn the business thoroughly; (3) As you learn, grow. Let's see how this simple program was followed very recently in the rapid building of a personal fortune.

Leland F. worked as a security officer in a branch of a large department store chain that went out of business, leaving him abruptly jobless. Unable to find similar work nearby, he began thinking about going into business for himself.

"At first I thought of starting a guard agency," Leland recalls, "but then I realized there was too much competition for that in my area. Finally I hit upon the idea of teaching businessmen how to prevent thefts. I knew that a large part of any store's profits are eaten up by shoplifting losses."

Leland was convinced the idea was a good one, and he followed the three basic steps for converting any good business idea into a big profit-making business.

Here's what Leland did:

He tested and developed his idea. He decided that anti-shoplifting methods are best taught in person, rather than through books or self-study courses. He knew that business seminars have become big business these days, with clients paying $100, $200, and even $300 for one or two days of instruction in something they need to know. To test and develop his seminar teaching skills, he decided to teach some free adult education classes for businessmen at a local public school.

He learned the business thoroughly. The anti-shoplifting classes in the adult ed program helped Leland develop the basic curriculum. Then he was ready for his first commercial seminar. He rented a meeting room in a hotel in a nearby city and sent out notices to retailers throughout the city. He limited the number of participants to 40, at $100 per person, and his seminar was fully booked two weeks in advance. He grossed $4,000. With $450 taken out for expenses, Leland's net profit was $3,550 for the one-day course.

As he learned, he grew. Leland began scheduling similar seminars in other cities, and he achieved similar success. And soon he learned that one venture can breed others. He had kept the names and addresses of all his seminar participants, and his next move was to sell them a monthly newsletter informing them of the latest store-security techniques.

Leland's organization expanded from seminars to newsletters and, lately, to seminars and publications on other business topics. Leland has built an organization of full-time and freelance instructors and consultants working in many parts of the country.

His specialty is prevention of shoplifting, but his initial profits enabled him to hire other specialists in other business fields. He has built a respected and highly profitable business training firm. Just a short while ago, he turned down an offer from another company to buy him out for more than a million dollars.

HOW TO SPEED THE FLOW OF PROFITS

No one has yet discovered an improvement on the old rules that the business that builds fastest is the one that offers quality and value. Throughout this book you see these two rules in action. But after you've developed quality and value, there are other profit-building techniques that can greatly add to your income.

So, starting with the two basics, let's examine some of the most powerful procedures being employed today. Here's what they are:

1. Provide quality
2. Offer value
3. Plow back your initial profits
4. Use specialized promotion techniques

It's a success formula that has worked repeatedly for entrepreneurs in all walks of business life. We'll examine the procedures one by one.

PROVIDE QUALITY

You'll remember that in the last chapter we discussed new twist opportunities. The people who used these opportunities are not imitators, they are *improvers*. In a phrase, they upgrade the quality.

Take bread as an example. Hundreds of companies make bread; some of it is pretty good. A few have offered outstanding quality, and they've been able to demand premium prices. Pepperidge Farm may come to your mind. An example you may not know about is the story of Mrs. Catherine Clark.

Mrs. Clark began her business with borrowed funds (a mortgage on her home plus $500 loaned by friends) and built it into a multi-million dollar enterprise expanding through many states.

The idea for her Brownberry Ovens, Inc. came to Mrs. Clark when she discovered that a small local bakery was producing an especially delicious and nutritious whole wheat bread. She was quick to spot the profit opportunity in mass-producing the same high quality.

Her initial borrowed funds paid for buying the recipe and some equipment from the other bakery, taking ownership of an old beer truck for deliveries, buying a vacant store in which to do the baking, and financing the early months of operation.

Mrs. Clark was right in assuming that people would love her bread. And she used intelligent expansion techniques by developing a line of related products. But the fact remains that her fortune was built on quality; yours should be also.

OFFER VALUE

The United States has seen hundreds of thousands of home builders come and go. But never has it seen anyone equal the achievements of Bill Levitt. His Levittowns made home-buying more affordable in America than ever before.

His company prospered because it offered unusual value. He achieved this by developing mass production techniques—just as Catherine Clark developed mass production techniques for her high-quality bread.

Before Mr. Levitt entered the picture, most homes were built on a board-by-board, nail-by-nail basis. He discovered ways of erecting entire sections, such as framing walls on the ground and then raising them into place.

This enabled the Levitt enterprise to build homes at attractive prices, capturing a sizable part of the post World War Two housing boom. The momentum continued to carry the company forward for years afterward.

The moral:

Develop new ways to offer value and you can beat out the competition.

This book is loaded with new ways you can offer value. Latch on to just one of them, combine it with your own business plan, and you could well have the start of a fortune.

PLOW BACK YOUR INITIAL PROFITS

At first this may puzzle you. You ask: "How can I speed up the flow of profits by putting them back into my business?"

The answer is leverage. You learned in Chapter 3 that a little money can be used to make a lot more money; there, we were talking about other people's money. But now, after you've started your business, you can multiply your profit-power by reinvesting some of your own income.

Certainly, use part of your new income to improve the quality of your life. But in the early months of profit-making, put the bulk of it back into the business to help it grow faster.

In my recent book, *How to Make Big Profits in Service Businesses* (Parker Publishing Co., Inc., West Nyack, N.Y. 10994), I relate the experience of a Long Island man who launched a successful mail order printing business. Sam W. had long been a boating enthusiast, and after his first year in business he found himself with a bank account of $15,000. It would have enabled him to trade in his boat for a new 30-footer.

Sam mulled it over, trying to decide whether or not to buy the new and larger boat. He also realized that with a larger printing press, he could expand his output, greatly increasing his capacity and his profits.

Sam's decision was in favor of the larger printing press, and it was a wise choice. It was the start of major growth for his company. And here's the outcome: Just two years later he was able to buy a 53-foot yacht for a quarter of a million dollars.

If he had bought that 30-foot boat, he wouldn't have expanded the business (or at least not for some time), and he might never have become the millionaire that he now is. He doesn't think two years was too long to wait for a boat that cost $220,000 more than the one he had originally wanted to buy.

Here's what plowing back your initial profits can do for you:

- Allow quick expansion
- Save on tax payments
- Make your business more secure
- Build a far bigger fortune

The second item, saving on tax payments, can provide you with double leverage. You've already used leverage to go into business, of course. If you were now to put all of your profits into your pocket, you'd naturally have to pay taxes on them. But the profits you plow back into the business are tax-free, providing you with windfall investment cash. It can be like having the government as a financial backer.

Multi-millionaire Harvey Schuster, who started in a $100-a-week bank job in 1959, and then parlayed $5,000 into a conglomerate of business and investment-related firms, could be in a very high tax bracket. But he succeeded in reducing it by reinvesting some of his excess cash. He says it would be self-defeating to let the government take more than half of his money. And he's right.

USE SPECIALIZED PROMOTION TECHNIQUES

One of the most widely read magazines in America—in fact, in many parts of the world—is the *Reader's Digest*. People and organizations seeking publicity would do almost anything for a favorable mention in one of its articles or columns. With its vast readership and esteem, you might think this magazine would have little or no need to promote itself outside its own pages.

But the fact is that the Digest employs some of the most sophisticated self-promotion techniques you'll see anywhere today. Contests, computer letters, newspaper advertising, and a continuous public relations effort have all helped this Pleasantville, N.Y., corporation multiply its own profits.

If those who run the *Reader's Digest* think *they* need promotion techniques, then the average business firm needs them ten times as much. You can have a great product or service, but unless people know about it they'll continue to pay for the inferior output of your competitors.

Promotion, much of it costing you next to nothing, can do great things to advance your business and your fortune.

It can be as simple as a slogan. ("Avis tries harder.") It can be as complex as those individually typed *Reader's Digest* computer letters. ("Dear Mr. Gillicothe: You may have won $10,000!")

If you need further proof of why promotion is needed for any business undertaking, consider this: At the same time that P.T. Barnum was luring millions of people into his show tents to see freaks and curiosities, Alexander Graham Bell couldn't get anyone to believe his telephone was worth bothering with. One man was a promoter and the other was not.

FREE WAYS TO GAIN ATTENTION

Some of the biggest deals have been closed as the result of free publicity obtained by the owner of a product or service. Free publicity is yours when you arrange for:

- Press releases
- Column reviews
- Trade directory listings
- Radio and TV interviews
- Tie-ins with a public service
- Photo coverage

These are just some of the self-promotion techniques you'll learn in Chapter 10. There's nothing like free publicity to speed the profits of any business enterprise.

THE FAIL-SAFE PROGRAM FOR LIFETIME WEALTH

There are two powerful rules for building a lifetime of prosperity based on your own initiative. Those who followed them have become rich and remained so. Those who ignored them have found little or only fleeting success. Here are the rules:

(1) **Never give up on a good idea.**

(2) **Adapt your plans to meet changing circumstances.**

Briefly, let's see what adhering to these rules can do for you.

NEVER GIVE UP ON A GOOD IDEA

It was economic wizard Roger Babson who called persistence "a great gold mine," and he couldn't have chosen better words. If Alexander Graham Bell had surrendered when people laughed at his invention, somebody else would have come along with the telephone and made a killing. If Howard Johnson had not nurtured the idea of highway restaurants, he might have retired as the owner of a small town tobacco shop.

"But," you inquire, "how do I know if my idea is really good enough to pursue?"

The answer is this: *It's good enough to pursue if it fills an important need.*

The dictionary defines *need* as the lack of something essential, desirable, or useful. Thus, filling a "need" doesn't mean we have to confine our money-making pursuits to re-inventing the wheel. Today's complex and affluent society has countless other "needs." Ponder these examples:

Essential: Food, shelter, clothing, health.

Desirable: Entertainment, hobbies, popularity, personal possessions.

Useful: Transportation, education, communication, self-improvement.

I'm sure you can think of numerous other items to be listed opposite the categories *essential*, *desirable*, and *useful*. The point is that if your Big Idea fills a need (or a lack) in any one of these categories, it is worth pursuing.

Ask yourself this question:

Does my product or service fill an important need by providing something essential, desirable, or useful?

And remember that the need doesn't have to be universal. It may exist in just one locality, or in one type of endeavor. There were already hundreds of thousands of city restaurants when Howard Johnson opened his on the highways. Bread was already a common household item when Catherine Clark began baking a product of higher quality.

And so, I repeat: If your Big Idea fills an important need, never give up on it. Pursue it and success has to follow.

ADAPT YOUR PLANS
TO MEET CHANGING CIRCUMSTANCES

We humans have yet to find a way to prepare totally accurate forecasts of what the future will bring. And so when I advise you never to give up on a good idea, I also must caution you to be sufficiently flexible to meet changing circumstances.

When World War II came along, Bill Levitt had to halt the home-building business that he had launched in the 1920's. The government put a stop to nearly all construction that was not related to the war effort. So what did he do? He got a government go-ahead to build homes for military officers, near an important base. He adapted his plans. And he did so well that, after building 750 homes for the military, he got approval to build twice as many for civilians employed by the military.

I have a friend who built a highly successful hamburger stand on a major highway. Highly successful, that is, until McDonald's put up one of their fast-food outlets across the way. So what did my friend do? He adapted, and converted his building into a full course restaurant. He made more money than ever, and now operates four other restaurants as well. I haven't seen his ledgers, but I'm sure he's well on the way to becoming a millionaire.

It has happened many times: Changing circumstances can present new opportunities you never dreamed of—making your Big Idea bigger than ever.

EXAMINE THESE MILLION-DOLLAR ACTIONS

There's a seven-letter word that is vital in building and holding onto your multi-million dollar empire. The word is **control**. Remember it well, as you vow always to:

- **Control** the ownership of your businesses.
- **Control** your expenditures.

- **Control** the actions of your workers.
- **Control** every move you make.
- **Control** the future of your empire.

Here are specific ways you can make **control** work for you:

Control the ownership of your businesses. In searching for other people's money to finance their businesses, many would-be wealth builders let control slip from their hands by granting investors too big an interest. Always use OPM only to the point where you continue to control the operation, and the profits, of your undertaking. That way, *you* make the decisions and will never have to give in to the dictates of outsiders who know far less about your field than you do.

Control your expenditures. Following the first blush of success, too many wealth-builders use much of their newfound cash to make foolish expenditures. Fancy office buildings, frilly corporate aircraft, and lavish luxuries often eat up money that should be applied in meaningful ways to expand the size and scope of the business. Other expenditure mistakes: putting incompetent friends and relatives on the payroll, allowing employees to waste time and money, permitting company facilities to be put to personal use. You'll have plenty of time and wherewithal for some of these indulgences later, after your fortune is safely in hand.

Control the actions of your workers. An entrepreneur can become so involved with the big picture that he tends to ignore routine actions by members of his staff. Mistakes pile up, and before he knows it, his empire is dwindling. It's right and proper to delegate authority to knowledgeable people but keep constant tabs on what they're doing, because much of what they do will either add to, or remove from, what's in *your* pocket.

Control every move you make. The bootstrap millionaire rarely makes a move in which he doesn't have the upper hand. His deals, loans, mergers, acquisitions, and stock sales are all designed to advance *his* fortune—not somebody else's. If this sounds hardhearted, remember that if the other guy is worth his salt, he's doing the same thing!

Control the future of your empire. Concentrate on one step at a time, but be aware of what your next steps will be. As explained in Chapters 1 and 2, have your plans in writing and refer to them and/or revise them as you progress. Keep tabs on changing trends that open up new and unexpected opportunities for profit.

Keep **control** and you will guarantee instead of gamble with your success. Some of the most powerful techniques for giving yourself a surefire guarantee of mounting riches are contained in the next chapter.

8

How to Test Your
Wealth-Building Plan

When you go into business, don't count on being lucky. If you were to depend on luck to build your fortune for you, you'd open the Yellow Pages of your phone book to a page at random, close your eyes, drop your finger to the page, and then choose a business based on the category where your finger fell. You might—just might—succeed, but the odds would be against you.

In fact, if you learn just one thing from this book, I hope it's this rule:

The odds are against the person who depends on luck.

"But," you ask, "aren't many of the people who have become self-made millionaires lucky? Hasn't luck played a role in making them rich?"

Certainly. But that's only because they have created the circumstances that allowed luck to take its course. One of this nation's best known early businessmen, Benjamin Franklin, said: "Diligence is the mother of good luck."

And the "diligence" we're going to be talking about in this chapter is *testing*. What appears on the surface to be the "luck" of an SMM has been, most often, the result of diligent testing. All

major moves, and many minor ones, are tested before they are
taken.

GUARANTEE—DON'T GAMBLE WITH—
YOUR SUCCESS

Proper use of the testing techniques explained in this chapter
will enable you to move ahead with confidence toward achieving
your multi-million-dollar goal. That's because testing:

- Allows you to pick the most effective methods for building
  your business and your fortune
- Tells you in advance just what kind of success you can expect
- Saves you money that might otherwise be wasted in pro-
  ceeding full-blast with procedures that turn out to be un-
  profitable
- Increases your income by demonstrating the most profitable areas of your business plan

Although some people may believe SMMs have achieved
their wealth through lucky hunches, you can be sure that any
hunches have been backed up with careful testing.

SMALL-SCALE TESTING—BIG-TIME PROFITS

Among other things, W. Daniel Renn had been, by the time
he reached his mid-twenties, a teacher and a salesman. He liked
selling best, but he was a man in search of a product. And finally
one day he discovered what he thought might be "the" product. It
was a fire alarm that his father-in-law had purchased for his home.

You are, of course, familiar with the great demand for home
fire alarms that exists today, but Daniel Renn was aware of what he
thought would be the potential demand more than a decade ago.
Call it a hunch if you must, but he didn't leave it at that.

He knew that fire alarms should be self-powered to be really
effective, because many fires go undiscovered until long after the
electricity goes off. And that's what attracted him to the product
that he discovered in his father-in-law's house; unlike most fire

alarms of the day, it did not have to be plugged in to the house wiring. This particular early model was activated by pressurized gas that was released by high temperatures, sounding a horn.

So Renn visited the factory where the product was made and he obtained the rights to peddle it in a territory surrounding his home city. He called on 20 homeowners and made sales to each. And as he did this, he worked on his sales demonstration, cutting it down from an initial hour to about one-third that length.

He continued selling the items at a highly successful pace, and soon he added salesmen to his staff. He taught them the selling techniques he had learned and honed.

In its first full calendar year of operation, Renn's firm achieved sales of nearly one-third of a million dollars. The year after that, sales increased to a million and a half dollars, and volume has continued to multiply ever since. Renn Enterprises soon had *thousands* of salesmen working for it, selling not only fire alarms but other safety products as well.

Daniel Renn literally tested his way to a fortune. Let's take a brief, but closer, look at how he did it.

FOUR STEPS TO AN EMPIRE

As you've seen, these four testing steps played an invaluable role in building Daniel Renn's business empire:

1. Immediately after obtaining the rights to sell the product in his area, he conducted a personal, small-scale test to see how it would go over with the buying public. The results were positive.

2. As he continued selling, he perfected his selling techniques, developing a sales method that could be followed by any competent salesman.

3. Once the techniques were perfected, he began to hire salesmen, teaching them the methods he had found to be most effective. The success of the first group of salesmen led to hiring a larger number.

4. With the success of the initial product, he expanded his product line as new items were tested and proven salable.

In Daniel Renn's case, all of the major tests listed above

proved positive. But testing can be equally effective in ruling out methods that at first appear to be good, thus saving you a lot of time and trouble, and allowing you to concentrate on the procedures that are really workable.

USE THE COMPARISON METHOD

In my book, *Second Income Money Makers* (Parker Publishing Company, Inc., West Nyack, N.Y. 10994), I relate the experience of a couple who were prevented from entering a wrong business thanks to testing.

One form of learning customer reaction to a business idea is to determine if *other* companies are already doing what you envision, and to find out how well they are doing. Bill and Flora Y. had an idea for a paperback bookshop in their community of some 5,000 residents. Knowing that the market for paperbacks was tremendous, they felt that they should be able to share in some of the profits being made.

But Flora told me, "We looked at all the towns within a 15–20 mile range of ours and couldn't find one paperback bookshop. This led us to wonder *why*. And, of course, we came up with the answer. People don't usually go out *looking* for paperback books the way they go out to buy a loaf of bread. They buy them on impulse when they happen to be in a drug store or at the newsstand."

Bill and Flora found that only in larger communities and shopping centers do paperback bookshops have a virtual guarantee of success—and only there because of the great numbers of passersby who step in from the sidewalk and buy on impulse.

This research spared the couple from entering a business that was bound to fail, but it led to one that was bound to succeed. Bill takes up the story:

"People do run out to get a loaf of bread or a carton of milk. Flora and I noticed a growing number of convenience food marts located in areas where houses and apartments are situated close together. Supermarkets on the highway and in shopping centers are fine for the weekly shopping trip, but when people need staples such as bread, butter, and eggs, they'll happily pay more if the little store is located just around the corner."

Bill and Flora picked a busy corner that didn't have such a

little store, and met with so much success that they've launched a chain of such outlets.

HOW TO KNOW IN ADVANCE
JUST HOW WELL YOU'LL DO

You've seen examples of the two basic methods of testing a new business plan in advance:

1. Daniel Renn conducted a small-scale version of his bigger plan when he went out to sell fire alarms to 20 homeowners. Results provided him with the positive go-ahead signal.

2. Bill and Flora Y. made what I call a Comparison Survey to determine how other companies were faring. This ruled out a bookshop but ruled *in* a convenience food mart.

You can apply one of these methods to gain an indication of how successful your own business plan will be. Which method should you use? It depends on the type of business you're considering. We'll take each method individually and see how it can be applied.

HOW TO USE SMALL-SCALE TESTING

As you've seen, Small-Scale Testing involves taking a sampling of your potential customers and actually offering your product or service to them. This is a crucial test that proves to you, right in the marketplace, whether or not people are willing to fork over hard cash for what you're offering.

Mail order companies, for example, almost always test their sales literature by mailing it to a small list of people. The percentage of the orders they receive from the test mailing is a good indication of how the offer will do when sent to a much larger group. If, say, a few thousand test pieces indicate that 3 percent of those receiving the ad actually place orders, a company can be fairly sure that a similar percentage will buy when the ads are mailed out to hundreds of thousands of people.

It's important to bear this rule in mind:

Small-Scale Testing works best when you are dealing with an individual product or service, but it is not practical when your business will handle a broad range of products or services.

Why is this? It's because you can easily conduct a consumer sampling of one item, but if you're planning to sell many items, too many tests or surveys would be involved.

Thus, if you plan to start a magazine, it would be practical to give it a consumer test because you can actually mail subscription offers to a sampling of people for whom the publication is to be published. But if you plan to open a magazine *store*, selling a broad variety of publications, your best testing method would be a Comparison Survey. (More on that later.)

ADVANCE TESTING PAYS OFF

At this point, I'm sure you have a question. "How," you ask, "can I test an idea for a magazine before going to the actual trouble and expense of writing and printing the magazine?"

The answer is simple. *Don't* write it or publish it, at least not until your tests prove positive. It is common business practice for the nation's largest corporations to make offers they are not yet ready to fulfill. They ask for orders, but not money, explaining that the customers will be billed later. If money is sent, it is immediately refunded.

If, on the other hand, the product or service you want to sell is something already produced by another company (with you acting as an agent) there is no problem in fulfilling orders received during your test. Daniel Renn didn't manufacture his fire alarms, he sold them for somebody else, and so his first twenty sales were real sales.

"All right," you say, "I get the general idea of how Small-Scale Testing works. Now give me some specifics on where it can be applied."

The best way I can provide the specifics is to offer these examples:

- You have invented an innovative product. Let's say it's a device that turns down your stereo or TV when the phone rings. You don't want to go into production until you know it will sell, so you make test offerings to consumers or department store buyers.

- You want to lead a tour to the art capitals of Europe. But before you make travel and hotel bookings, you need an idea of whether or not people will sign up for it. You do some test advertising.

- You've found a company that manufactures a handy new office machine. You'd like to start a regional dealership selling that machine, but first you want to know if office managers will buy it. Thus you obtain a sample or two and make the rounds demonstrating the product. You'll soon have a good idea of how it will sell.

- You've worked out a highly efficient method for handling the bookkeeping chores of small businesses. But before buying the mini-computer you'll need, you want to determine the market for your service. So you actually offer it to a sampling of small businesses. If you're concerned about creating ill will by not being able, immediately, to provide the service you have offered, you can conduct the test in another city or territory. Money never actually changes hands, because at the point of contract-signing you politely back out, saying you have decided after all not to offer the service in that area.

Please remember these two points:

1. It is not dishonorable to offer a product or service you don't have. This kind of testing is constantly being done by many of the nation's largest, most respected business firms. As long as no payment is accepted, no one has been hurt.

2. In many cases, you actually *can* follow through by providing the product or service during the test period. Daniel Renn did actually sell fire alarms during his early sales tests. And in the final example given above, you could actually provide the computerized bookkeeping service by either (1) leasing a computer or (2) renting time on somebody else's computer.

This leads us to a variation of the Small-Scale Testing

Technique. It can be explained in this statement:

If for any reason you don't want to offer something you can't actually provide during the test stages, offer a closely similar product or service that you *can* provide.

Here are a few examples of how you can conduct what I call "substitution tests."

- Although hoping eventually to lead your own tours of the European art capitals, you conduct your testing by selling an existing tour provided by another company. You do it on a commission basis.

- You have an idea for writing and then selling a "how to" construction manual through the mail. Before printing and offering it, you test your idea by buying a somewhat similar book at wholesale from another publisher. You then sell *that* book to determine the market.

- You'd like to start a home insulation firm, but want to test the idea before loading up with equipment and supplies. What you do is work out an arrangement with a reputable company already in the home insulation field; your sales are referred to them. (It's interesting to note that many of the nation's leading department stores that sell home installation services actually farm the work out to independent contractors.)

HOW TO CONDUCT A COMPARISON SURVEY

Although Small-Scale Testing works fine with an individual product or service, when it comes to the type of business offering a broad range of products or services, a Comparison Survey is your best bet.

It would not be practical, for example, to do small-scale testing to determine the need for such things as, say, a motel, a fast food outlet, a travel agency, or a housing development.

You certainly shouldn't go out and build a motel or start a travel agency until you have some pretty positive indications that you'll find enough customers to make it worthwhile. And it would be awfully hard to "test sell" motel space or a broad range of travel services without the actual motel or travel agency to back you up.

So how *do* you determine if the area needs what you have in mind? You look for similar businesses and you follow some rules of thumb to determine if there's room for you, too.

COMPARISON SURVEYING MADE EASY

The big established companies have it down to a formula. A franchised chain of motels or hamburger stands knows the amount of highway traffic that is needed to make a branch profitable. It knows just where to locate the branch in any given community. It knows all this from experience, and it has the facts and figures in its own guidebook, as a matter of policy.

So how does the newcomer learn where to locate his motel or hamburger stand or what-have-you? He lets the established firms do most of the picking for him.

Here's what you do:

1. Check the locations of the established outlets. Make a list of all within a certain radius; say, 25 miles.

2. Note all the particulars of that location to determine just why it was picked. It may be at the crossing of two major state highways, or perhaps it's near an Interstate exit. Or, if it's a retail store, it may be located in a sizable shopping center or a busy downtown area.

3. You might take an informal traffic count. During two-hour periods on several different days of the week, count the passersby (cars, if it's a drive-to type of business, pedestrians if it's in a pedestrian shopping area).

4. Search for a location with similar traffic conditions that does not yet have an establishment of the type you want to open. This location must be no closer to competing firms than the existing companies are to each other.

You will also want to do some research in books and manuals on your chosen field. Often these include criteria on choosing a location that is most likely to be successful. Check a large library's business section, and also obtain some inexpensive U.S. Government publications.

The Small Business Administration has two catalogs listing

helpful business publications: SBA-115A, which lists currently available free publications, and SBA-115B, listing for-sale booklets. Write or visit the nearest SBA office or contact its main office, Washington, D.C. 20416.

HOW TO KNOW IN ADVANCE JUST HOW WELL YOU'LL DO

The two methods of testing a projected new business— Small-Scale Testing and Comparison Surveys—can give you not only a clear signal as to whether or not to proceed, but they can also give you a good indication of what income to expect.

With Small-Scale Testing, you use multiples to make your financial projection. If, for example, a mail order company makes $100 on 30 sales to a test list, it can anticipate making $10-million when it conducts a full mailing to a similar list 100,000 times as large. If you succeed in selling 40 foreign tours during your first test, you can expect to sell an equal number in similarly-promoted tour packages that are offered later.

Of course, Small-Scale Testing requires that you actually carry out a part of your business plan. If you want an indication even before doing that, you can make a Comparison Survey. Keen observation can tell you how well competing businesses are doing. You may not be able to hone it down to the last dollar, but it's easy enough to detect whether a motel is nearly filled every night or whether a fast food outlet is pounding out the hamburgers continuously. And, seated at a table, leisurely eating a hamburger of your own, you can take a fast count of the volume of sales during various quarter-hour periods.

Thus, Comparison Surveys give you an idea of potential, while Small-Scale Testing puts your idea right on the line, resulting in hard-dollar figures.

THE TESTING PROCESS NEVER ENDS

If you think that once you've successfully tested a new business product or idea the testing is over and done with, think again. Just take a look at business giants such as Sears Roebuck,

McDonald's, and A&P. Like most major corporations, they still test major moves before making them.

You might think that a leader in its field such as Sears wouldn't have to test. You might think its executives would *know* what new products will sell, and how well they'll sell. But executives of major corporations are the first to admit that they rely heavily on testing. What does it do for them?

- It *saves* millions of dollars for their companies by avoiding full-scale introduction of products the public simply doesn't want—products that seemed to hold a lot of promise when studied by the "experts" in the business.

- Testing has *made* millions of dollars for companies by telling them what the public does want and by giving these companies the foresight to promote those products heavily.

If McDonald's wants to introduce a new product in its restaurants, it is tested first in one region. If successful there, it is introduced throughout the system. Sears often uses the same type of region-geared approach. A new product is introduced at several key stores. If successful there, it is offered system-wide.

What these firms are doing, in essence, is Small-Scale Testing. If it's important for a well-established business, think how much more important it can be for testing a business idea before a company is even launched.

THOMAS EDISON'S BIG FAILURE

The inventions of Thomas Edison led to the formation of a number of giant corporations, but the invention that won him his very first patent was a failure.

It was not a failure mechanically, mind you, because his vote-recording machine worked well and efficiently. It was designed for legislative bodies such as the U.S. Congress. Young Edison took it to Washington with high expectations that it would bring in the money he badly needed. Leaders in Congress agreed that it worked well. But they didn't want it. They explained to Edison that the slow, old-fashioned method of vote-counting gave them time to negotiate on important pieces of legislation, and they didn't want to lose that advantage by introducing a speedy mechanical device.

This taught Thomas Edison an important lesson that was to make him a successful person and inventor throughout the remainder of his career. He made himself a promise never again to invent anything that was not wanted and that was not needed by the public at large. And that, of course, is what testing is all about.

MAGIC INDICATORS FOR BUILDING A FORTUNE

Testing provides you with what the head of one giant corporation calls "magic indicators." Frank L. tells me that the major part of his success in the appliance manufacturing industry has been due not so much to his own ability, as to where testing has led him to use his ability.

"Many is the time," Frank recalls, "that I have compiled an exhaustive business plan for a new product only to find through testing that some of the procedures won't work very well and that other procedures I hadn't even dreamed of would work much better."

GET YOUR PILOT PROJECT STARTED NOW

O.K., you've had a business dream for years. You're pretty sure it can make a lot of money for you, but something has been holding you back. You don't want to make the investment (or arrange the borrowing) required, and you don't want to give up your present steady employment, until you *know* the plan will work.

And you won't know the plan will work until you try it. And that, of course, leads to the old vicious cycle. You don't dare do it unless you know it'll work, and you can't know it'll work unless you do it.

So, *test it!* Don't quit your job, don't take out a big bank loan, don't go into it full scale. Test it with a pilot project. And the time to start is now.

Let me tell you about the pilot project conducted by the founders of the firm that makes Adolph's Meat Tenderizer. Larry Deutsch and Lloyd Rigler discovered the tenderizer in a Los

Angeles restaurant where it was used by the chef, Adolph, to make the more inexpensive cuts of steak tender. Deutsch and Rigler realized that the same tenderizing process would be a boon to housewives, making it possible for more Americans to enjoy steaks at home more often. They wouldn't need the expensive cuts to have juicy, tender servings.

So this enterprising pair obtained the rights to package and sell the product using Adolph's name, and they offered it for sale by demonstrating it to customers in a local department store. This was their pilot project. The customers quickly bought out their entire supply.

With the success of their pilot project, Deutsch and Rigler realized they had a winner on their hands. Now they knew they could proceed full steam ahead; but they didn't. They took time out for more testing; testing to improve the product formula; testing to develop better sales techniques.

And then, when they did offer it on the market, their testing continued. This is when their *sales* testing became of increasing importance. Successful sales methods developed in the Los Angeles area enabled them to enlarge their territory until it reached a nationwide scale.

And testing of new product lines has allowed the firm to enter other food-related fields, expanding sales and income.

HOW TO CONDUCT YOUR OWN PILOT PROJECT

Launching your own pilot project can be extremely easy. Just follow these rules:

- If it's a product you're featuring, have some samples produced and test-sell them either directly to consumers or to retail store buyers.
- If you're planning a service, offer it to prospects until you sign up a few customers. Then test it further by actually performing the service.

"Sure," you say, "that works fine with some things. But what if my plan is to build apartment houses? What do I do, build *one* apartment and offer it for rent?"

Hardly. But even in this type of field, you would do better by starting with a pilot project. Don't build a 150-unit building the first time out. Instead, put up an eight or ten-unit structure. What you learn by doing it will return tremendous dividends when you move into the really big time.

Remember:

- McDonald's began with one store.
- Howard Johnson started with an ice cream counter in a tobacco shop.
- Walter Chrysler got started by taking one car apart and putting it back together again.
- Conrad Hilton launched his empire with a tiny hotel in a small Texas town.

All of these were, in effect, pilot projects. But look what they led to!

The moral: Get *your* pilot project under way as soon as you possibly can. Whether it involves test-selling a new product, opening a prototype store, offering a business service, or whatever—don't put it off. The quicker you put your plans in motion and into the testing process, the quicker you'll find the best means of building your million-dollar empire.

9

Enhance Your Fortune With People Leverage

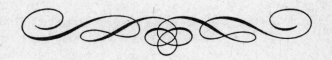

Can you identify the common factor in the fortune-building stories of Alexander Graham Bell, Henry Ford, and Polaroid founder Edwin Land? Each of the above people used People Leverage to build or enhance his fortune. The fact is that most self-made millionaires couldn't have gotten where they are without People Leverage.

USE YOUR BRAINS AND THEIR BRAWN

What is People Leverage? It works much the same way as leveraging money. You leverage money by using a little of your own money to reap the benefits of a greater amount of money put up by others. With People Leverage, your own effort is multiplied many times by the efforts of others.

For example, the shoemaker of olden times couldn't make a great deal of money because there is a limit to how many shoes one man can manufacture. Then along came a smart shoemaker who decided to put a lot of apprentices to work and produce a lot more shoes. The more apprentices he had, the more shoes his operation could produce—and the more money he could make. This was an early use of People Leverage.

The same principle is still being applied today, but in a more sophisticated manner. Today's wealth-builder knows that a good idea becomes a lot more profitable once you've picked the right people to carry that idea out for you.

There are limits to your time and even to your talent. But, with People Leverage, you have unlimited time and talent at your command. It can make you a millionaire in short order.

"MR. WATSON, COME HERE, I WANT YOU"

It's ironic that the first seven words uttered by Alexander Graham Bell on the telephone also spelled out one of the secrets of his success. For the truth is that Bell was clumsy with his hands. He was to become one of the world's most famous inventors, yet he had to depend on others to carry out his ideas. In this case, it was a model-maker named Thomas Watson. Later, in other projects, he enlisted other persons with expertise in whatever field he happened to be engaged in at the time.

Alexander Graham Bell knew the value of People Leverage. In fact, he probably never could have succeeded without it.

HOW TO LET OTHER PEOPLE MAKE YOU RICH

Starting from scratch—armed only with a good money-making idea—you can use People Leverage to build your own financial empire. Strong statement? Perhaps, but it's being done every day. Here's what People Leverage can do for you:

- Provide you with instant knowledge it would take years to acquire on your own
- Multiply your productive capacity overnight
- Place at your disposal specialized talents you could never personally acquire
- Allow you to carry out a complicated money-making project with ease
- Build a fortune much more rapidly than would otherwise be possible.

Let's take a look at each of these benefits and see how it can be applied by you:

GAIN INSTANT WEALTH-BUILDING KNOWLEDGE

Many excellent ideas are conceived by people who don't really know how to carry out those ideas. In most such cases, the ideas are therefore quickly abandoned. But not always.

Take the case of John C., who spotted a need in his home town for a local radio station. The area was served only by a metropolitan station located some 40 miles away, and the station was too large to pay much attention to John's home town. Very little local news was broadcast, and the advertising rates were far too steep for local businessmen.

Trouble was, John didn't know the first thing about electronics. Not a person to let such a minor drawback hold him back, John enlisted the aid of a science teacher at the local high school, who was also a ham radio operator and a licensed engineer. John told his partner, "You handle the technical details, and I'll take care of the business aspects."

So While John C.'s partner worked on finding an open spot on the radio dial and applying for a license with the FCC, John began to drum up business support in the local community.

"Yes," you say, "but what about people to staff the radio station—professional announcers and newscasters?" Again, People Leverage to the rescue. Ads in the professional trade magazine, *Broadcasting*, brought them hundreds of job applications.

The upshot is that this one little local radio station was the start of a chain of stations that eventually also included TV outlets and more recently has moved into Cable TV and publishing as well. John C. is a multi-millionaire.

Starting from scratch, as John did, you can gain the expertise of others. If at first you can't afford to hire people with the needed knowledge, then "partnerize" it. Give an expert a share of the pie. If the idea is a good one, there's plenty for both of you.

MULTIPLY YOUR PRODUCTIVE CAPACITY OVERNIGHT

The shoemaker who spends his life slaving alone at his last manages to eke out an existence; the one who enlists apprentices often gets rich. There is, after all, a limit to what you can do alone, and that's why this chapter will show how you can easily gain the work and talents of others in amassing your million-dollar fortune.

Catherine Clark learned the technique early in her career as founder and owner of Brownberry Ovens, Inc. She faced the necessity of increasing the price on one of her product lines. At that point, the company could not afford to toss out its supply of containers that had the old price printed on them.

Mrs. Clark decided that the only solution was to re-mark the existing containers. With a limited staff, she clearly needed to multiply her productive capacity overnight, even if only on a temporary basis. So what did she do? She enlisted the aid of a church women's group, promising to donate $1100 to the church if the ladies would embark on a project of placing new price stickers on the existing wrappers.

It is, of course, rare for most business people to have to resort to such an emergency procedure—even though, in this case, Mrs. Clark achieved the re-labeling at considerably less than the cost of producing new wrappers. But the principle she employed—People Leverage—is vital to the success of any business enterprise that depends on productive capacity. For the fact is this:

> **As long as there is demand for your product, your profits can increase with each additional person you can put to work producing that product.**

In other words, each additional productive employee on your staff means more dollars in your pocket. That's why this chapter will explain the many ways you can reap giant dividends from making proper use of People Leverage.

TAP A RESERVOIR OF SPECIALIZED TALENTS

A third benefit of People Leverage is that it greatly increases the range of abilities and talents at your command. Rare is the businessperson who is jack-of-all-trades when it comes to knowing the many facets of carrying out his or her money-making ideas. The founder of a high-potential special interest magazine may, for example, know a lot about editing manuscripts, but far too little about selling advertising or preparing page layouts. What does such a person do? Call upon the talents of others, naturally.

That is, indeed, just what Phil L. did when he founded a

magazine designed for specialty manufacturers. Phil had worked as a public relations man for various manufacturing firms and he knew the industry well. He also knew that there were many companies ready to advertise in a magazine distributed just to manufacturing firms.

So his idea for a trade publication was a natural. Being in public relations, he knew he could come up with the editorial material. But what about the advertising, and the technical expertise? His solution was to convince several other persons with the needed talents to buy into his organization. They became partners and co-workers. Their magazine was an instant success, and it has since led to spin-off money-making projects such as an expensive newsletter and a series of training seminars sold to subscribers.

CARRY OUT A COMPLICATED MONEY PROJECT WITH EASE

Henry Ford developed his first automobile in a lonely pursuit. But the growing popularity of his product quickly made his enterprise increasingly complicated. It's one thing to build a prototype car; it's another to mass-produce it on a profitable scale.

His eventual solution was to make highly effective use of People Leverage by introducing the *assembly line*. By taking the car parts to the workers, instead of the workers to the car parts, Henry Ford got more production per employee. Everyone benefitted. Cars were produced more inexpensively, he paid unusually high wages for the time, and, of course, he profited handsomely from all this.

Just as the manufacture of automobiles includes many different processes, most modern businesses involve many different tasks. Rare is the person who can carry out each with equal ease. That's why today's entrepreneur turns to experts to do what he cannot personally do himself.

When Andrew T. began a mail order business dealing in leather goods, he knew a lot about his product, but little about the business. His use of People Leverage included paying a copywriter to prepare his ads, a letter shop to prepare his catalog, a mailing list broker to recommend lists, and an advertising agency to arrange for ads in the periodicals.

"Too many people starting out in mail order," Andy says, "try to do it all themselves, and they make a lot of costly mistakes." His use of experts brought rapid success to his enterprise, and as you might expect, he has long since become an expert in all of its phases.

SPEED UP YOUR FORTUNE-BUILDING PROCESS

Imagine if Andy had gone it alone. He might eventually have made it, but each of his mistakes would have cost him both time and money; and, as many other people have done, he might have given up in bitter disappointment. Fortunately, his wise use of People Leverage prevented that.

"Production of our leather goods began as a family project," Andy recalls. "My wife, Theresa, our two kids, and I were all involved. But when the orders began piling up, we soon learned our limitations. We were inundated!"

So Andy hired piece workers to assemble products in their homes from the leather pieces he and his family cut out for them.

"Our production capacity multiplied overnight," he explains. "And soon I was able to rent a building and hire full-time workers." His plant, since expanded several times, now includes not only production facilities, but a sizable mailing department and even a retail outlet.

Andy learned early that once there was a demand for his product, each employee he hired to help meet that demand increased his level of profit.

"I pay fair wages," he points out, "but I also receive profit for each employee I hire. Let's say I pay John Jones $5.50 an hour. That means in addition to the $5.50 I'm paying him, I'm earning maybe a dollar an hour in extra profit, because Mr. Jones is providing me with merchandise I otherwise wouldn't be able to offer to the public."

HOW TO PUT EXPERTS AT YOUR COMMAND

Let's assume that you've hit upon your million-dollar idea, a plan you're convinced can and will work—if only you had the specialized knowledge required to carry it out. Ah, and there's the rub; how can you get all the know-how required and still implement the idea before somebody else with a similar brainstorm comes along and beats you to the punch?

The answer, of course, is People Leverage. You can use it in any of these four ways to capture the money-making knowledge you need to carry out your business idea. Here are the four methods to consider:

- Pick a partner who knows the ropes.
- Hire an expert in the field.
- Retain a consultant to get you started.
- Farm out the complicated tasks.

We've touched on some of these techniques in the case histories related so far in this chapter. But let's examine them a bit more closely with an eye toward how you can put them to use.

PICK A PARTNER WHO KNOWS THE ROPES

Most often, when a person with a business idea decides to take on a partner, it's for the investment the partner provides. But sometimes it makes just as much sense to pick a partner on the basis of the knowledge and experience he can devote to the business.

"Since he has the needed expertise, and all I have is the idea, what's to prevent him from going ahead with my idea on his own, once I have explained it to him?" That's a question I'm often asked when I speak of the benefits of "partnerizing" special know-how.

For a partnership to be of benefit to both parties, each person must make an important contribution. If one partner's role is providing the needed knowledge, the other's may be in the form of time to carry out the business idea, or money to use in getting it started. Often there is a sharing of these roles.

I know of a partnership that illustrates this point perfectly. When the CB radio craze hit the U.S. back in the mid-1970's, Dorothy L. recognized it for what it was—an excellent money-making opportunity. Her idea was to open a store specializing in CB radios and related equipment. She had a few thousand dollars to invest and knew there were several vacant stores in nearby highway shopping centers. The problem, naturally, was that Dorothy knew next to nothing about how CB radios operate.

"I realized that for a CB store to be successful, someone in management would have to know how to pick the best brands, and of course how to repair those that were returned for service. My contribution would be my time and my talent as a salesperson."

So what did she do? Dot set out in search of a partner who could provide the knowledge she needed. She could have hired a technician and left it at that, but Dorothy wanted more than a repairman; she wanted someone to help her make important decisions based on technical expertise.

Besides, her goal was the eventual ownership of not just one, but a chain, of CB stores. And the most important move she made toward achieving that goal was to locate a knowledgeable partner through a classified ad she inserted in the Business Opportunities section of the local newspaper.

Dorothy's partner put up part of the money for the first CB outlet. She agreed to work full time in the store while he came in evenings and weekends. The arrangement was so successful that, within six months, he quit his job and went to work for the partnership full time. They achieved their goal of a regional chain of stores even more rapidly than Dorothy had anticipated.

HIRE AN EXPERT IN THE FIELD

Sometimes it makes more sense to "hire" the technical knowledge you need than to sign it on as a partner. This occurs:

- When you only need the technical assistance to get started
- When you need experts in several categories
- When the technical requirement is relatively minor compared to the overall business plan

The point is not to let a good business idea slip by merely because you don't have the specific knowledge needed to put it in action making big money for you. Too many people are floored by what they imagine to be awesome technical details.

Experts don't usually come cheap, but in relation to the money they can make for you, the price can be surprisingly low. Did Alexander Graham Bell take on Thomas Watson as a partner, merely because Mr. Watson knew how to build gadgets and Bell was all thumbs? I've already told you the answer to that one. It's the Bell Telephone System, not the Bell-Watson System.

RETAIN A CONSULTANT TO GET YOU STARTED

Smart wealth-builders are never afraid to ask for help when they need it. They realize their own limitations and are aware that, in order to make the most of their business plans, they must go out and buy whatever expert knowledge they need.

You wouldn't think of prescribing your own medicine for a serious illness any more than you would try to be your own lawyer in a complicated court case. Unfortunately, many people who know enough to hire experts in the field of medicine and law think they can embark on a complicated business scheme without the professional advice of those trained and experienced in the field.

How can you obtain such professional advice? In any of several ways:

- Check trade groups, trade magazines, and professional societies for the names of consultants in the field.
- Sign up for one or more seminars conducted by recognized experts in the type of business you've chosen.
- Seek advice from non-competing businessmen; those whose firms don't deal with the same customers you'll be seeking.

We live in an age of specialization. Eventually, you'll be an expert in your chosen field. But before you reach that point, you'll benefit greatly from the experience of those who have gone before you. This, too, is a form of People Leverage.

FARM OUT COMPLICATED TASKS

Too many people pass up excellent money-making opportunities because the idea they have in mind seems too complicated. Either they don't have the training or experience to carry out the project, or they lack the time to do it adequately. They have the mistaken notion that just because they're starting small, they have to do everything themselves.

Not so! The wise wealth-builder is the person who knows when it is more practical to assign certain tasks to outside workers or agencies. Even the nation's largest corporations are not entirely self-sufficient. They stick to what they know best, hiring "expertise" when it would not be practical or economical to do it themselves. Thus, the "Big Three" auto makers hire advertising agencies to help tout their products, concentrating their own efforts on design and manufacture; magazines turn the subscription fulfillment process over to companies set up for just that purpose.

The beginning wealth-builder can and should do the same thing. If, for example, you launch a mail order enterprise, there is no reason why you should prepare your own advertising copy if ad-writing doesn't happen to be one of your specialties. The cost of hiring a professional to do a better job will be returned to you many times over in the form of increased sales.

DON'T SPREAD YOURSELF TOO THIN

On the other hand, like Elsie Pollock, you may have the ability to handle all of the tasks required in your project, but realize that to do everything single-handedly would be to spread yourself too thin.

Mrs. Pollock was college-trained as a dress designer, and it is in that field that she has become a millionaire. She started with a $500 investment; her idea was maternity dresses. She was the first to introduce really practical clothing for pregnant women. She got the idea when she spotted her pregnant sister wearing a wraparound that did nothing for her appearance.

It might seem that someone getting started with a minimal investment such as Mrs. Pollock's would decide to make her own dresses—at least at the beginning. But this entrepreneur knew that her efforts should be concentrated on obtaining sales outlets for her products. So she hired a local seamstress to carry out her designs. Her business took in $100,000 the first year, and it hit the million-dollar category not long after that.

So remember this rule:

By using People Leverage to farm out certain tasks, you can concentrate on the money-making aspects of your business that really do require your personal attention.

Unless you have all the time in the world, don't try to do everything by yourself. Wise use of People Leverage will allow you to concentrate on converting your beginning business into a burgeoning empire.

HE IGNORED THE OLD-TIMERS

"Old-timers said leasing trucks would be too expensive. Fortunately, I was too busy building a multi-million dollar company to listen." So says 26-year-old Irwin Carasso, who built Tree of Life, Inc. from a one-man health food distributorship into one of the largest corporations of its kind in the country.

You might think that a company whose main business is delivering food to the stores would run its own trucks. But not Carasso's firm. His deliveries are made with trucks leased from Ryder Truck Rental, Inc. Carasso explains: "Sure it costs money. But it would cost me a helluva lot more to own my own trucks. And I could never run them as well."

This highly successful SMM knows the practical and financial advantages of leveraging equipment as well as people. "With Ryder, I have $750,000 worth of equipment on the road that didn't cost me a penny in capital outlay. My money and my time go into my health food business instead of into trucks."

If Irwin Carasso's experience proves an important point, so does the experience of the company from which he leases his vehicles. When you reach Chapter 11, you'll learn how you can benefit from the experience of SMM Jim Ryder.

HOW TO GET WORKERS WITHOUT SPENDING A CENT

"Sure, it's fine to advise someone to hire outsiders to carry part of the load, but I have very little cash to invest." That's the kind of reply I often get when telling clients about the advantages of People Leverage.

And my reply is that in some cases, you need not spend a cent of your own money. In fact, whenever you can, you should let the customer carry the load! Here are some of the ways this can be accomplished:

- If your basic product or service is produced for you by outsiders, hire only enough workers to keep slightly ahead of customers' orders.
- Pay salesmen on a commission basis so that the money they receive comes directly out of what the customer pays you.

- If your business involves anything that is made-to-order for your customers, require them to make down payments or deposits to cover the cost of materials and labor used in filling their order.

In 1947, Edwin H. Land had developed, at least on paper, his 60-second Polaroid Land Camera. But it was going to take more than a third of a million dollars to produce it—something his little company didn't have. What did Land do? He farmed out the work to an outfit willing to do it on a handshake and the promise that it would get the manufacturing contract for the first 10,000 cameras.

To this day, the Polaroid company adheres to a People Leverage policy of not manufacturing any items that can be purchased on the outside at reasonable cost. Its film-base, for example, is obtained from one of its competitors—Kodak—and as well from du Pont.

Daniel Renn, the man who built his fortune by selling home fire detection systems (you met him in an earlier chapter) made effective use of People Leverage by building a giant sales organization. True, he did the initial selling himself, but that was to perfect the sales techniques. He followed this up by instructing his sales personnel in these techniques and then letting them carry the bulk of the load. You've already learned what People Leverage did for him.

EXAMINE THESE OUTSTANDING PL OPPORTUNITIES

Opportunities to make highly profitable use of People Leverage exist in just about every business field, but a lot can be learned by looking at some of the prime examples. Outstanding PL opportunities can be found in such fields as:

Mail Order: Here's a business that can be run virtually from start to finish with People Leverage. Your ads can be prepared for you by professional copywriters who know from years of experience what will pull orders and what won't. You need never handle the products you sell; they can be "drop-shipped" directly from the manufacturer or distributor to your customers. Mailing lists for sending out sales letters are readily obtainable from scores of list brokerage houses. The actual printing and stuffing of envelopes?

This, too, can be handled for you by outsiders—so-called "letter shops" geared to deal with just such work.

Sales Organization: Some of America's richest entrepreneurs have made their fortunes by building an organization of sales personnel. First the entrepreneur finds a "hot" product line, and then he or she develops an effective sales method. After that, a sales staff is recruited with the pay coming almost, if not entirely, out of commissions. The key advantage: for every sale made by a member of your staff, you earn a substantial cut. The more salesmen you have, and the more products they sell, the more you make.

Service Agency: Business services comprise one of the most needed and most profitable money-making opportunities available today. Virtually every business needs services of various types, ranging from office cleaning and floor waxing to providing temporary personnel and repairing office or industrial machines. The person who sets up a business service agency hires people to do the work for him; or a prototype business is established and the experience gained in running this "pilot project" helps the entrepreneur set up a nationwide network of franchised service agencies. You've already read about the great success achieved by such people as Walter Kelly and H&R Block.

Education: The public schools and the colleges of the nation don't begin to fill the tremendous demand for education. Providing education in specialized subjects is a highly profitable field. You hire instructors on a part-time basis—when and as needed—to teach the students who have signed up in your commerical school. Many commercial schools teach the same subjects as the public schools, but their methods of teaching are different, being geared to the special needs of their clientele. Thus, French and Spanish may be taught in just about every public school in the land, but most large cities also have a branch of the commercially-operated Berlitz School of Languages. Why? Because Berlitz stresses conversation and rapid learning rather than the traditional and tedious "learning by the rules" method.

GO NATIONWIDE

In two of my most recent books, *How to Make Big Money in Service Businesses*, and *Second Income Money Makers*, I give dozens of examples of how People Leverage can be used in starting a

sales, service, or education-oriented business. The emphasis in
these books is on starting one such enterprise, and the two books
go into quite a bit of detail on how to do it. But why stop at one? As
you know, the emphasis in the book you are now reading is on
earning really big money—in the million-dollar category—so one
lonely service or sales agency won't do. But a nationwide network
will, and the way to start is with a prototype, or pilot project.

It's important to remember this fact:

**If you can run one business profitably, you have the know-
how to operate dozens or even hundreds of others just like it
in other locations.**

And that, my friend, is the key to getting rich in the sales,
service, or education field, using People Leverage.

PEOPLE LEVERAGE BUILDS
A MILLION-DOLLAR FORTUNE

Martin D. had worked as promotional director for a medium-
sized corporation in Chicago, spending a lot of his time preparing
trade show exhibits and conducting seminars for customers so they
could make better (and more) use of his corporation's products. He
earned a top salary, but he also realized that he was earning more
money for his employer than for himself.

"I knew that if I were to show other companies how they could
use the same techniques I had been using for my employer, I could
make really big money," Martin explains. This prompted him to
establish his own business in the trade promotional field.

"But to go nationwide," he explains, "I needed a big staff—
something I couldn't afford at the outset." So, People Leverage to
the rescue. How? He recruited sales personnel on a commission
basis. He trained people how to locate and sign up small and
medium-sized customers anxious to have their trade show promotions conducted for them by experienced professionals in the field.
And Martin had no problem in finding part-timers to work under
the guidance of his managers in setting up and running the trade
show assignments he received.

Now, some two years after its start, Martin's company has
scores of sales and operating experts. It performs a valuable func-

tion for many customers who, in the past, had not been realizing the full potential of trade show presentations.

"I expect to gross more than three-million dollars this year," Martin reports, "and this from a business I began on a shoestring." It it weren't for People Leverage—obtaining salesmen who worked on a commission basis, and hiring personnel locally on a daily fee basis for each trade show assignment—it wouldn't have been possible.

HOW TO GET WORKERS
WITHOUT SPENDING A CENT

As you've seen in this chapter, each person you have working for you—helping provide a product or service you can sell, or actively involved in the selling of the product or service—increases the amount of money you can personally make. And when you have little money to invest toward getting a business started, People Leverage becomes even more important. Many of today's wealth-builders have found ways to build a starting staff without any cash outlay at all.

Here are some of the methods they've used, and which you, too, should consider.

- Retain sales personnel on a commission-only basis.

- Hire temporary or part-time workers—people who work to fulfill specific customer orders.

- Offer an interest in the business to individuals who have the time and ability to perform needed functions.

- Start with a franchise arrangement in which you supply others with the business plan and supplies to conduct the enterprise on their own.

- Contract for outside services to be used only when and as needed.

You should realize that the payroll is often the heftiest expense in any business. Any way you can minimize it—and still maintain output and quality—will help you achieve your profit goals with greater speed. And many people have found that the best way to achieve this is through People Leverage.

THE ULTIMATE USE OF PEOPLE LEVERAGE

Would you believe that one person, having absolutely no employees, can run a multi-million dollar corporation alone? I didn't until I met Beatrice N., the owner of a cosmetics supply firm in the east. Bea started out by working as a salesperson for one of the home party outfits that recruits women to invite friends into their homes and demonstrate beauty products.

Bea earned fairly good money working for that firm, but soon realized that by improving on its methods—and offering better products obtainable elsewhere—she could do better. So she wrote to a number of manufacturers, put together a product line, and then began advertising in some of the women's magazines. She recruited hundreds of women from coast to coast, and provided each of them with printed instructions on how to conduct home sales parties successfully.

The women she recruited bought kits of sample products to demonstrate at their parties. Then they sent their orders in to Bea, who arranged to have the manufacturers drop-ship the items directly to the retail buyers.

Bea is still using this basic method, although now she hires the services of a mail order fulfillment firm that ships the items under her company's mailing label.

"Any services I can't actually provide myself are contracted to outside companies," Bea reports. "It works perfectly for me, because I pay only for work actually performed and for products that customers have already ordered."

Bea admits she may be a People Leverage "fanatic"—that at this point it might be more economical to set up her own office and warehouse—but since People Leverage has worked so well for her until now, she has no plans to change her methods in the near future.

START USING PEOPLE LEVERAGE TODAY

Right now, even before you've started your first money-making enterprise, you can make excellent use of People Leverage. How? Let other people guide you to the fortune you seek.

You don't know what kind of business you'd like to start?

Examine the success stories of self-made millionaires, and gain a wealth of ideas.

You aren't sure of how to launch the kind of business you've chosen? Visit existing businesses in the field and see how they've done it. And send for a free copy of the *Business Planning Guide* by David H. Bangs Jr. and William R. Osgood, available by writing to the Federal Reserve Bank of Boston, Boston, Mass. 02106.

You don't know where to raise the needed capital? You can get free advice by reading the publication, *SBA Business Loans*, available free at the nearest office of the Small Business Administration. Also, the Bank of America, Department 3120, PO Box 37000, San Francisco, Calif. 94137 will send you a free list of helpful publications that can do a lot to get you started.

Using free advice available from the many sources mentioned in this book is an important way to put People Leverage to work for you.

And in the next chapter we'll be talking about another powerful form of leverage—self-promotion. For some of today's SMMs, it has been the one most important factor in building their fortunes.

10

Promote Your Way
to Prosperity

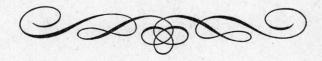

He's a born promoter! How many times have you heard or read that about somebody who has pulled himself up from nowhere and become a self-made millionaire?

There may be "born" promoters, but self-promotion is as much a skill as a talent, and the purpose of this chapter is to teach you that skill. Once you have the ability to promote yourself and your ideas, the road to riches becomes a lot easier.

HOW TO BUILD A BIG NAME FAST

The best idea or business plan in the world is of little good unless people are willing to pay for it—and they can't pay for it until they know about it. That's why promotion is so important, especially at the beginning when your company has not yet built a base of satisfied customers who can spread the good word.

Building a "big name" fast can help you win success rapidly. How do you do it? Here are some of the methods we'll be discussing in this chapter:

- Use attention-getting techniques to gain free publicity.

- Build personal contacts that attract riches.
- Gain fame through association with big names.
- Create a clamor for your product or service by providing it to a few key people who will rave about it.

These are just a few of the techniques you'll learn—techniques for building the kind of big name that will get your enterprise off the ground rapidly, headed toward the million-dollar empire that you seek.

HOW TO GET FREE PUBLICITY

Paid advertising is great—when you can afford it. But what about the guy or gal who is at the earliest stages of empire-building? Without much of an advertising budget, you need all the free publicity you can get. Let me tell you about Jim C., who was thrust into riches thanks to the free publicity he arranged.

A long-time amateur dog breeder, Jim spotted the need for guard dogs to help stave off burglaries in the medium-sized city where he lived. He'd been involved in training dogs for friends, and he had taught obedience classes. So he had the basic knowledge with which to launch a business in breeding and training—and then selling—guard dogs.

Jim made a modest amount of money at the start by inserting classified ads in the local newspapers. But his ambition was much greater than that. He decided that publicity could propel him into a bigger financial sphere.

He got the idea of contacting his customers to determine just how well his animals had performed "on the job." He was told of several instances in which one of his "trainees" had been effective in preventing robberies or cornering the culprits until police could arrive. Armed with this information, Jim wrote up an item for the newspapers in the form of a press release. People are always interested in reading about animals, and Jim was right in expecting the papers to print his release.

PUBLICITY BREEDS MORE PUBLICITY

The item in the papers caught the eye of a dog columnist, who did an extensive write-up of his own featuring Jim's dog-training methods. This publicity led to invitations for local radio and TV interviews, and even to an appearance on a network show, demonstrating one of his animals as it went through its paces.

Seeking to expand beyond his local community, Jim opened a branch in a nearby city. In order to attract more attention to his new branch, Jim presented that city's police department with two fully-trained animals for use in their work. This naturally led to media coverage in that community, and to some attention-getting photo reports.

The result of the continuing publicity that he had arranged for himself and his animals is that Jim's business boomed. The second branch led to a third, and a fourth, and so on until he had outlets in 20 different states. And with each new location, he utilized the same free publicity techniques that had brought him his early success.

SIX KEY PUBLICITY METHODS

It's surprising how few businessmen take advantage of the free publicity that is theirs for the asking. It's really easy to get the kind of press and broadcast coverage that Jim C. got. Later on we'll be discussing some of the more high-powered attention-getting methods, but right now let's look at the "standard" publicity techniques that any business can use.

Press Releases: The kind of press release that gets printed is the one that tells of something out of the ordinary. Notice that Jim C. didn't send out a release merely stating that he was in the business of selling dogs; he related some examples of the feats his dogs were performing. Every business has at least a few interesting or unusual stories to tell, and these are the things newspapers are anxious to publish.

Column Reviews: More attention-getting than the average newspaper story is a mention in a feature column. Every newspaper publishes a number of such columns on various topics. If your product or service is in a field covered by a feature column, be sure to call it to the attention of the person responsible for writing the column. Again, bear in mind that it's the unusual or highly interesting that stands the greatest chance of getting published.

Trade Directory Listings: Just about every business field has one or more trade directories where potential customers look when seeking to buy a product or service in that field. Listings in many of the trade directories are free, but many businessmen surprisingly wait for the directory publishers to contact them. The smart entrepreneur seeks out such listings, knowing that the business it brings him is pure "gravy."

Radio and TV Interviews: Talk shows, expanded news programs, and public service broadcasts are all fertile ground for obtaining free publicity for your business. As with just about any kind of publicity, it's important to pick out a few intriguing aspects of your product or service—something that sets you or your enterprise apart from other businesses. (We'll be delving into specific attention-getting devices later in this chapter.)

Public Service Tie-Ins: Whenever your business can perform a public service, it is eligible for attention in the news media. Many businesses sponsor local athletic teams, but it is generally better to do as Jim C. did and have the public service directly related to what you're selling, because the publicity you get will call attention to your product or service. You'll recall that Jim C. donated two of his dogs to the local police department. The news items about this pointed up the value of his dogs in police work.

Photo Coverage: A picture is worth a thousand words, they say, and it certainly can be when the photo tells an interesting story related to your business. Newspapers are always looking for good photo material. The subject matter can be "gimmicky" (such as the time I checked in a huge turtle at a hotel to publicize the fact that it would be on display at a local trade show) or it can be what I call human-interest-factual. An example of this might be a picture spread of some disadvantaged youths receiving on-the-job training at your place of business.

THE VALUE OF FREE PUBLICITY

When you get your name before the public—and keep it there—it's your name that naturally comes to mind when people are in the market for the product or service you are selling. It would take an entire book (perhaps even a set of books) to outline most of the effective means that practically any business can use to keep its image favorably before the public. But I can and will give you a few key tips here, knowing that, once you begin using them, the experience will make you more alert to the other possibilities.

HOW TO PROMOTE A SERVICE BUSINESS

In a service-oriented business, it's usually your ability that the customer is paying for. Naturally, he wants to be assured that you can do the job. How can you convince him of this? Simply by establishing yourself as an authority. Thus, entrepreneurs in the service field work hard to gain reputations as authorities in their fields.

A friend of mine (I'm calling her Norma B. because for reasons that will become obvious, she wants me to give no hint of her real identity) knew the value of establishing herself as an authority even before she actually became one.

"I studied interior designing in college, and after a brief and unsuccessful career as a housewife, I decided to open my own business as a consultant. I'd had no real practical experience as a working designer, and I suppose it took a lot of gall to set myself up as a consultant to the rich and to large corporations. But I knew I had the ability—and I had the ideas that many of the tried-and-true professionals seemed to be bypassing," she recalls.

Without credentials to help her gain clients, Norma B. had to build a pedigree from scratch. Here are some of the techniques she used:

1. Norma got her first bit of publicity by writing a letter to the editor of the local newspaper criticizing the decor used in a recently-opened cultural center. She gave some ideas as to how it might have been done better, and in the letter she subtly let it be known that she was an expert. This was valuable free advertising.

2. She volunteered to serve on a local Board of Architectural Review. Although the board's main purpose was to approve building exteriors, she headed a subcommittee advising builders on interior designs. This, too, kept her name before the public.

3. Once her local practice was firmly established, Norma B. began to think of expanding to other cities. Needing a

regional, if not a national, reputation, she decided that the
best way to do it was through magazine articles. She
realized that "How To" articles giving helpful hints on
decorating would gain the widest audience. Not being a
particularly good writer, she engaged a professional to put
the prose together, working from outlines that she had
prepared. The articles, under her byline, were published
first in regional and then in national magazines.

4. Soon she was asked to give talks before organizations and
at conventions, and she was frequently invited to appear
on women's TV talk shows.

The result is that, within a period of two or three years, Norma
built a reputation as one of the nation's top experts on interior
design. Let me stress again that she had the ability to begin with—
it was merely public recognition of her ability that needed working
on. Work on it she did, and so successfully, that Norma B. is now
the owner of one of the nation's most prosperous interior decorating companies. The fees she charges are outlandish. But her waiting list of future clients keeps on growing.

HOW TO PROMOTE A
PRODUCT-ORIENTED BUSINESS

Gaining attention as the vendor of products—as opposed to
services—is usually a different ball game. While it is helpful to be
known as an "expert" who can give valuable advice to the purchasers of your products, most often you must think of other ways to
convince people to buy from you rather than from your competitors.

Lars T. was a small-time home-building contractor in the
northeast who decided to embark on the most ambitious project of
his life—a housing development. After he had obtained the needed
financing and had nearly completed his first model home, a mild
recession set in and the demand for new homes slackened.

"There was fierce competition among us builders, so I had to
come up with a means of getting what few home-buyers there were
to put my development on their 'must see' list," Lars explains.

So here's what Lars did:

1. Knowing that he had to get pictures of his model home published in the papers as frequently as possible, he volunteered to let it be used for the teaching of home economics classes given by area schools and adult education programs. Thus he cashed in on the fact that newspapers are far more willing to give publicity to institutions and organizations than to commercial enterprises.

2. Next came the task of convincing potential home-buyers that they simply had to stop by at his model home. His development was located about 25 miles from a major city, so Lars realized that many shoppers would be from the city and thus not familiar with his territory. His action was to advertise the fact that by visiting his project first, they would be given free road maps of the area, with all housing projects pinpointed on the map. Many businessmen would scoff at the idea of handing free publicity to competitors, but this builder knew that a home shown is a home half-sold; he left it up to his salesmen to do the rest when couples arrived to pick up their maps.

3. Seeking to draw attention to the beautiful view from his hilltop development, Lars invited students in a local art class to put the view "on canvas" as part of a competition. He bought the five best paintings for $50 apiece and then donated them to the County Home for Senior Citizens. This resulted in several of the paintings being reproduced in the newspapers, with the view being properly identified as the one that could be seen from Lars' development.

His promotional techniques paid off handsomely. Despite the recession, the project was completely sold out within six months. Lars T. was to become an SMM in what many consider to be a highly risky field, and he recognizes that promotion played a big role in his achieving success.

RULES FOR NAME-BUILDING

Profiting from the experiences of the three people mentioned so far in this chapter, we can now set down a list of basic rules for image-building in a service or product-oriented business. And here they are:

- Prepare press releases about unusual or highly interesting aspects of your business.
- Seek photo coverage whenever possible, because it naturally draws more attention.
- Capitalize on the fact that a tie-in with a public service will bring you publicity easier than practically any other technique.
- Establish yourself as an authority in the field. Get yourself quoted and interviewed as much as possible. This keeps your name before the public and also builds public confidence in you and your service or product.
- Use giveaways to get buyers to visit your place of business; such "premiums" need not be expensive as long as they are of value to the recipients.

USE PROMOTION FOR REPEAT SALES TOO

Once they win a new customer, many businessmen sit back and think the battle is won. But, when the success of an enterprise depends on customers returning again and again, promotion plays an important role.

As one highly successful self-promoter told me, "It isn't enough to provide your customers with good products or services; you have to keep *reminding* them about how well they are faring when they deal with you." Naturally, this isn't done with self-congratulatory back-patting. The methods are more subtle.

Winston Schuler, who built a small Michigan eatery into a multi-million-dollar restaurant empire, used many promotional techniques to achieve his goal. One technique: taking the trouble to learn the names and occupations of as many diners as possible. Then, when they return, most are welcomed by name—impressing them with their own importance.

But the technique that Schuler has employed most often, and in a number of different ways, has been to give customers even more than they have bargained for. They come in for a good meal (which they certainly get) but they leave with more than that. One time it may be a set of four cocktail glasses; another time it may be a birthday cake (if the occasion warrants). And diners get various food bonuses not listed on the menu—things such as hot garlic toast, special appetizers, and tasty cheeses. These serve as constant reminders that they get more when they buy meals from Winston Schuler.

HOW ABOUT PRICES?

At this point, you probably have a question. "Doesn't this cost more? How can you be competitive in pricing?" Certainly, providing premiums costs more. But very often your prices can be held at a competitive level because of the increased amount of business you have generated with the bonuses. It's the old maxim of "The higher the volume, the lower the price."

And what if you can't hold prices down? The fact that you charge more can sometimes be a plus, actually attracting business your way. Guard dog dealer Jim C. started out by charging the same for his dogs as competitors charged for theirs. Then, on a hunch, he tried upping the prices by about 10 percent.

The next article about his business that appeared in one of the papers stated: "This firm charges more for its guard dogs than do most other dealers in the region. But the proprietor explains that his customers are getting a superior animal, and one that is better trained." Jim's business picked up noticeably, and he has stuck to his higher price policy.

So remember this important promotional point:

When you're selling a product or service that is somewhat unique (not a mass-produced item available practically anywhere) you may be able to impress buyers with its high quality merely by raising the price.

This technique has worked for selling not only guard dogs, but also for selling such other commodities as art, architecture, handcrafted items, and surgical operations. Surgical operations? Certainly. Did you ever notice how the patients tend to line up for the higher-priced surgeons—or psychiatrists? It's not always because of the superior skills of those practitioners. Sometimes it's because their higher fees have convinced the public that their abilities must be that much greater.

SIZZLING TECHNIQUES THAT
SKYROCKET YOU TO FAME AND FORTUNE

My client listened patiently while I outlined much of what you've read so far in this chapter. When I reached the point you've now reached, he interrupted.

"All this is fine," he said, "for the person who is satisfied with starting small and then taking several years in developing his business. But I've got to be big from the start! If I'm slow getting off the ground, others can steal my idea and beat me to the punch."

There are, I told him, a number of SMMs who have achieved fame and fortune with tremendous speed using specialized techniques. But there is one requirement all of them had to meet, and which has to be met by anyone trying to follow in their footsteps. Here's the requirement:

You must have a solid business plan before you employ high-powered publicity techniques.

Why? Simply because if you gain a lot of attention from the publicity you've generated, and then fall flat on your face when it comes to *performance*, nobody will believe you or pay much attention to you in the future. They could even scoff at your future promotional schemes. So it's vital that you have a carefully-planned business program before you start using the high-powered promotional techniques you're about to learn.

THE SECRET OF HIGH-POWERED PROMOTION

The easiest way to obtain prime attention from the public and the news media, at minimum expense, is this:

Have others generate the promotion for you.

By this, I don't mean hiring a publicity agent. I mean tying your business plan in with some other existing "force" and then allowing that "force" to carry you on to fame and prosperity. The "force" of which I speak can take any of several different forms:

- Current headline events.
- Existing businesses

- A generated controversy
- Important personal contacts

I'm sure you'll want to know how any of these forces can get your venture off to a skyrocket start. So let's examine them one by one.

CASH IN ON HEADLINE EVENTS

When a topic is currently "hot" in the news, reporters can't get enough of it. They know the public has an insatiable appetite to learn all it can about the "hot" item, so story after story is generated in the press and on the airwaves.

Remember when the motion picture, *Jaws*, was released? There were more shark sightings reported in the media that year than in any recent year in memory—not because more sharks were actually seen, but because shark-sightings suddenly became "important" news.

It was the same with *Star Wars*. There was a sudden influx of reports from people who had spotted UFOs. In recent years, many people claimed to have seen UFOs; but such claims became a lot more newsworthy when science fiction emerged as a hot topic of current interest.

So how can a businessman profit from this? By spotting a topic that is receiving top press coverage at the moment, and then relating his promotion to that topic. Naturally, you can't pick just any hot topic. There has to be a general relationship between the subject and your business. But a little patience and a keen study of what is making news will lead you, before long, to an appropriate theme.

Some examples:

- When the TV series, *Roots*, was on just about everybody's mind, a book publisher re-issued a volume giving instructions on how to trace one's own family's roots. It became a top seller.
- When Jimmy Carter came into national prominence, peanuts became a theme of many new products. There were peanuts tee-shirts, peanuts pencil-holders, peanuts anything-you-can-think-of. The novelty wore off after a

while—but not until a lot of promoters had made a lot of money.

- When the Watergate revelations of two Washington Post reporters were much in the news, a small and struggling home study school teaching writing skills capitalized on the newfound interest in investigative journalism. Its ads, news releases, and letters to prospective students promised that they, too, could learn to be successful journalists. The school's enrollment doubled.

- It would be impossible to count the number of companies that have benefitted from the energy crisis. Hundreds of books have been published on the practical (and not so practical) means of generating your own wind and solar power. Products that used to be sold on the basis of their power or usefulness are now touted for their "energy efficiency"; a tiny New England company making wood-burning stoves had to expand three times in order to meet the sudden demand for its product.

TAP THE RESOURCES OF EXISTING BUSINESSES

The second "force" that can generate high-powered promotion for you is the business community itself. You can tap the resources of an established and influential business firm by making a deal that is mutually profitable. Get it to promote your product in a way that will benefit both of you handsomely.

You read, in the last chapter, of the deal made by the financially-strapped Polaroid company to get its first batch of cameras manufactured. Well, when it came time to sell what had been produced, Polaroid had little money for promotion.

Part of its answer was to work out a new type of deal, using the technique we're now discussing. It tied in with existing businesses, and got them to give it plenty of promotion. How? One large department store in each major American city was given exclusive rights to sell the product for one month if the store featured Polaroid extensively in its advertising. Also, the store was to promote Polaroid with big in-store displays.

The first such arrangement was worked out in Boston, and the arrangement exceeded the company's expectations. The stock was quickly sold out. Similar experiences followed in other cities—so much so that the manufacturer had difficulty keeping up with demand.

So plan to cash in on this fact:

When you show other business firms how they can profit from promoting your product or service, you can have their tremendous resources working for you.

Such activities are known as "promotional tie-ins" and they have become a common occurrence in today's business world. A number of today's SMMs couldn't have gotten where they are without promotional tie-ins.

GENERATE A CONTROVERSY—AND GET RICH

Sometimes it pays to become a troublemaker. So much so that this constitutes the third "force" you can tap in order to reap the benefits of high-powered promotion.

Get people to argue about your product or service and many of them will buy it. It's a technique that has been used time and again by the world's greatest promoters.

Fashion designers are well aware of this force, and they benefit from it greatly. Whenever one of them comes out with a controversial "new look" it receives widespread publicity. The fashion writers debate it in their columns, the photographers snap repeated pictures of the style, and people who like to be up-to-the-minute in their dress snap it up in the stores.

Here are some other ways that controversy has been used as a promotional tool:

A small company just starting out in the manufacture of high-speed power boats encouraged a public controversy over whether it was "patriotic" to buy its product, which was certainly not energy-conserving. Newspaper and magazine articles, noting that it burned more gasoline than most power boats, also pointed out that it was exceedingly fast in the water. This was just what the manufacturer wanted, and it resulted in thousands of sales to speedboat enthusiasts.

The owner of a fire alarm dealership got himself issued a noise pollution summons for testing his highest-priced alarm in the store at night. It seems that it woke up the entire neighborhood, and that's just what he wanted. Newspapers ran the story and described the shrill alarm. "The hundreds of systems I sold as a result of that publicity," he reports, "paid for the $25 fine a thousand times over. Buyers realized that if the alarm woke up the neighbors it had to be good."

Sometimes an advertisement can generate controversy and result in publicity worth much, much more than the cost of the ad. The owner of a book store knew this when he ran newspaper ads depicting a clerk in his store discussing a book with a customer—alongside another picture showing a bored clerk behind the cash register at a discount store's book department. The caption: "Where would you rather browse for books—where the personnel can discuss them with you intelligently, or where a gum-chewing ignoramus thinks the only kind of best-seller is the song she heard on the radio yesterday?" He mailed copies of the ad to the discount store clerks' union, and they filed the expected protest. As a result of the publicity, book-lovers began flocking to his store. Later, he toned down his ads, while maintaining the same theme. His new slogan: "A place where books, and readers, are highly respected."

There's an important rule you must follow when using the "controversy force" as a promotional tool:

The controversy you create must be designed to play up the appealing aspects of your product or service.

Examine this rule in action in the examples you've just read. The fashion designer draws attention to his modish styles; the boat manufacturer gains publicity for the high speed of his products; the fire alarm dealer gets a lot of tremendous publicity because his product is so effective; the book dealer, hurt by discount store competition, focuses on the special attention his store gives its customers.

So never create a controversy merely to gain notoriety. Do it in a way that makes people begin talking about the good points of whatever it is that you are selling.

MAKE CONTACTS THAT ATTRACT RICHES

A lot of people believe the old saying, "it's not what you know, it's who you know." I've never gone along with that, for reasons that should already be evident to readers of this book. All of the SMMs I've encountered created, developed, and carried out their own fortune-building programs. And the programs were top-notch to begin with, or they wouldn't have brought such top-dollar results.

On the other hand, it certainly doesn't *hurt* to know the right people. While making important contacts cannot by itself make you rich, it can greatly speed up your wealth-building program.

So the fourth and final "force" to tap in promoting your product or service is comprised of personal contacts. We'll be considering three types:

- Business contacts
- Group contacts
- Contacts among the famous

Let's examine these three categories to see how each can help bring you riches from the money-making plan you've developed.

PROMOTE YOURSELF THROUGH BUSINESS CONTACTS

The very first SMM you met in this book, back in the first chapter, was Meshulam Riklis, the 29-year-old immigrant who went from a $110-per-week job to controlling an empire worth hundreds of millions of dollars. He is, naturally, a man of many talents—but, do you know what one of his most important talents is? He builds close relationships with his business associates.

And what does that mean? It means having influential people ready, willing, and able to help you when you need them. In one of his business deals he worked with a couple of fellows who were influential in local financial circles. The deal benefitted all parties, and the two men became lasting friends of Riklis'. Later, they were able to introduce him to the owner of a large company that he wanted to acquire. That introduction paved the way for a multi-million-dollar deal that was important to Riklis' career.

"Yes," you say, "but how can I make such contacts in the first place? Especially if I'm starting from scratch?"

And therein, my friend, lies your answer. Just as you start your business empire from scratch, you develop your list of business contacts from scratch.

But this doesn't mean you have to start "small." Please recall the experience of Jerry Gordon, the man who worked in a Kentucky Fried Chicken store, the one who invented an automatic flour sifter. Where did he go for support? Right to the top: to Col. Sanders himself. And as you read earlier, the Kentucky Colonel recognized the value of the product and readily lent his support.

HOW TO BUILD BUSINESS CONTACTS

Rule Number One for building contacts that can help you in business is to be where the people you need are. Why do you think that so many businesspeople in any given community join the so-called "service" organizations? To be of service to the community? Well, that might be a small part of the reason, but their main motivation is to get to know people who can help them in their business.

Randall P. had started, and was successfully operating, a small company providing computer services for other small firms. His initial success gave him the ambition to open up a number of branches. But to do that, he needed a major loan. Having developed a friendship with the head of the local bank, by serving on some service club projects together, he was able to outline his plans to the banker in a friendly, informal manner. The loan was offered, and Randall's empire was well on its way.

Rule Number Two is to develop and maintain good working relationships with your customers—and even your competitors. Randall P. profited from this repeatedly. "I always tried to go the extra mile in serving my customers," he remembers, "giving them a bit more than they had bargained or paid for. You'd be surprised how many of them recommended my service to their friends and associates, and this brought me a lot of new business."

How can competitors help you? During extremely busy periods when Randall was unable to accept any extra assignments, he made a practice of giving the business to a competitor who was able to handle it. "I received tremendous dividends from this,"

Randall reports. "The competing firms began to throw a lot of business my way, and it was an important factor in building the large corporation I now own."

These two rules for building business contacts are so important that I'm going to re-state them:

1. Do everything you can to develop friendships with important people who can be helpful to you in the future; do this by joining the clubs they belong to, volunteering for the service projects on which they work, and aligning yourself with the causes they support.

2. Build a bank account of "favors" owed you by doing favors for the people who are important to the future of your business. This "you scratch my back, I'll scratch yours" policy can bring you far greater dividends than your initial "investment."

In other words, doing a small favor for a business acquaintance can sometimes result in a far bigger favor being done for you in the future. Although many people think machines have taken over, human contacts are still the major driving force in the business world.

BUILD GROUP CONTACTS

Business contacts need not be confined to individuals. Some of the best promotional contacts involve entire groups of people. As you'll see, the groups don't have to be formal organizations; they can be people who fit into one category or another.

For example, one of the early promotions for the Polaroid Land Camera involved the "category" of person who vacations in Miami. The Polaroid promoters reasoned that if vacationers in the Sunshine State could be convinced to try and to buy the camera, they'd show it off when they returned home, and this would give the camera exposure all over the country.

Here's how they conducted their promotion: a group of attractive young women, and a similar number of lifeguards, were provided with the camera that developed its own pictures. They were told to snap pictures of vacationers on the beach, and then give each vacationer the picture that had just been taken of him or her. As you might imagine, these well-to-do tourists were fascinated by the product, and they soon bought up all the Polaroid cameras that were available in the Miami-area stores. Upon returning home, each naturally demonstrated his or her marvelous new contraption to friends and relatives.

Thus, for the cost of a relatively few cameras, Polaroid had achieved nationwide promotion, with thousands of people serving as its willing promoters.

How else have group contacts been used in business promotion? Here are some examples:

> The product is donated, or provided at reduced cost, to an organization in exchange for public acknowledgment. (Every program printed by New York City's Metropolitan Opera carries the statement: Knabe Piano used exclusively.) Those who belong to, or attend functions sponsored by, the organization repeatedly see the product name and naturally associate it with the organization itself.

> The product is sold in volume to fund-raising organizations which re-sell it for profit. (Girl Scout cookies are an example.) This not only brings immediate sales, but it also exposes the product to consumers who may never have purchased it before. When it comes time for "refills" they often look for it in the stores.

> Manufacturers often sponsor contests or tournaments in a field closely related to their product. The resultant publicity can be worth far more than the cost of the promotion.

Entrepreneurs realize that associating their product or service with a highly-regarded organization or group of people is one of the most effective means of promotion available to them. By doing this, they have all the members of the organization working for them as "good will ambassadors" and their company name is spread far and wide.

MAKE CONTACTS AMONG THE FAMOUS

When your company reaches the multi-million-dollar stage, you can afford to hire TV stars and famous athletes to speak for it in advertisements. But even long before this happens, you can still make, and benefit from, contacts among the famous.

Book publishers, even little ones, do it all the time. They send review copies of a new work to famous authors, asking for their comments. Those remarks are then quoted on the jacket and in advertising for the volume.

"I understand how this can benefit them," you say, "but I'm going to run a hamburger stand. How can I make, and profit from, contacts among the famous?" One thing you can't do is name one of your hamburgers after a famous movie star. After hearing of it, the personage could turn around and sue you—and collect.

But here's what hamburger vendor Sanford T. did, something you could do also: Sandy sponsored a charity day on behalf of a local orphanage, pledging to donate the day's proceeds. He wrote to a well-known motion picture performer who lived in the area and got the star to appear at his stand on the day of the event. This brought a lot of attention to his business before, during, and after the affair. He has made it an annual thing, picking another star when the initial one is not available.

In fact, it's a standard operating procedure at all of Sandy's food outlets. (Thanks to his successful use of the Success Repetition Factor, and high-powered promotional techniques, he now owns a chain of hamburger stands.)

MAKE OTHERS HAVE TO SAY "YES"

Having important contacts is half the ballgame. The other half, and indeed the winning half, is getting them to do your bidding. How do you get them to want to do that? By demonstrating to them how it will benefit them, either financially or emotionally. Going back over some of the examples we've encountered in this section on using contacts, let's examine what motivated the people involved.

Miami tourists were thrilled at "discovering" a brand new type of camera, and they rushed to show it off to their friends.

Non-profit organizations are always in need of assistance, and will almost always provide publicity for a company that can help them out.

Unlike athletes, famous authors have not yet come to realize that their names are worth money, and so they endorse other people's books willingly and freely. (They may also be hoping for a return endorsement the next time one of their own books is published.)

Most people—even famous people—like to be known for the good deeds they do. That's why Sanford T. is so successful in getting them to endorse, and appear at, his charity days.

Randall P., the owner of the small computer firm, got his first big bank loan not merely because he had met a banker in the local service club, but because he was able to follow through on that friendship by showing the banker that the bank would have a safe and profitable loan with Randy.

To boil it all down to one paragraph, people want to do things because they will get something out of it. That "something" may be hard cash, or it may merely be self-esteem. But, as one highly successful promoter told me, "No one does anything for nothing." To put it another way: Provide them with what they crave, and you'll have their support.

USE YOURSELF TO PROMOTE YOURSELF

You, yourself, are one of your own best "contacts" when it comes to promoting additional business. Once your company is established and has developed a number of satisfied customers, you can generate spin-off profits by selling new products and new services to those same customers. And that's what the next chapter is all about.

11

Reap Extra Windfalls With Little Effort

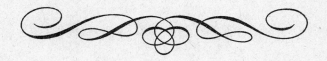

When you go into business, plan on making it three or four businesses. By this, I don't mean starting three or four different companies—I mean having your one company, no matter how small or large it is, sell a lot more than its main product or service.

For the fact is, that once you are in business, wonderful opportunities exist for little-effort, big-profit sidelines. Customers who came to you to buy one thing often wind up buying several other items, and people who have no need for your main product or service are attracted by your sideline offerings.

THE KEY TO ADDED PROFITS

As a common example of sideline opportunities being pursued to the hilt, think of the corner drugstore. Pharmacies used to stick pretty much to medicines. But over the years they have offered more and more products, until today, most of their business comes from selling non-medicinal items. Walk into the typical American drugstore and you'll see that it resembles a five-and-ten much more than a place for dispensing drugs.

Even supermarkets are getting into the act. First they added women's magazines, then household utensils, and now some are getting into appliance sales, offering such things as TVs and refrigerators. When you subscribe to the *Reader's Digest* or to *Time* magazine, you are immediately put on their mailing lists to receive offers for their books and records.

So if some of the nation's biggest firms are not satisfied with the profits earned from their main endeavor, why should you be? The answer, of course, is that you should not be. And this chapter shows how you can reap big windfall profits from sidelines to your main business, no matter what it happens to be.

HOW ONE VENTURE BREEDS MANY OTHERS

Many small businessmen get into sideline ventures quite by accident, but you should plan on it even before you hang out your first shingle. It may take bicycle repairman John Doe several years before he realizes that people who bring their bikes to him are prime candidates to buy accessories—if only he had some on display to be purchased on impulse by those who visit his shop. In the meanwhile, he has lost several years' worth of windfall profits.

The great advantage of most sidelines is that they cost very little to operate. In our John Doe example, his only added cost would be the wholesale price of the accessories that he places on display. Since the items are sold to customers who are already in his shop, there's no added outlay for advertising.

Even when a sideline venture does cost money to implement, it costs far less than if you were to start from scratch, launching it as an entirely new business. That's because, as an established business-person, your name is worth money. In fact, that's what you are cashing in on—your name, your reputation, and your group of satisfied customers.

SPIN-OFFS CAN MEAN BIG BUSINESS

When Long Island housewife Jean Nidetch founded Weight Watchers, she had little idea of the business spin-offs it would generate. But the name Weight Watchers became so well known, it would have been poor business not to capitalize on it. And capitalize on it she did—coming forth with cookbooks, dietary foods, and a magazine.

When Kemmons Wilson launched the Holiday Inn chain of motels, he might have had some idea of the spin-off possibilities, because he'd operated a number of businesses previously. But I'm sure he didn't know just how vast his sideline holdings would become. As you learned in Chapter 2, the Kemmons Wilson empire now encompasses such fields as transportation, health care, home furnishings, manufacturing, computer technology, and construction. It's worth well over a billion dollars.

The whole idea of this book is to have you start out doing what existing self-made millionaires had to learn from experience. Since nearly all SMMs have eventually learned they could profit handsomely from sideline ventures, this is something you should plan on doing right from the start.

MAKE MULTIPLE SALES TO THE SAME CUSTOMER

"Related sidelines, I call them." So says Roy L., speaking of the spin-off ventures he launched after building a successful swimming pool dealership. "I soon realized that homeowners who bought my in-ground pools were proud of their properties. So it was a natural for me to go into the lawn maintenance business."

Roy built a good starting customer base for his lawn enterprise from among the people who'd bought his pools. While surveying their properties for the best pool location, he'd make a practice of commenting on the obviously fine appearance of their grounds. He would also note that, what with the new pool and all, they might not have as much time to keep the lawn in such good shape; then came the plug for the lawn maintenance service.

"And you know," Roy muses, "it works two ways. Now that I'm also getting business from non-pool-buyers, I frequently am able to sell pool installations to my lawn customers!"

Actually, it works four or five ways. Roy has expanded his holdings to include (1) an aluminum siding operation, (2) a storm window undertaking, and (3) a "dormer" firm that specializes in building small additions to private homes. His net income amounts to more than $200,000 per year, and the value of his companies is well into the millions of dollars.

HOW TO MAKE YOUR NAME
WORTH A MILLION DOLLARS

Regardless of the initial business field you enter, you can do as Roy L. did and make a fortune selling extra products and services to your customers. Based on his experience, here are the guidelines that can steer you to your own fortune:

1. Pick what Roy calls a "related sideline." It doesn't have to be in the same field; it merely has to be a product or service that would appeal to the same type of customer. Fertilizing lawns is hardly the same field as installing swimming pools, but the same homeowner is a likely prospect for both types of endeavor.

2. Offer quality and value in whatever you do. This is because a satisfied customer is the best candidate for becoming a buyer of the other items you sell.

3. Use the same, or a similar, name in each of your enterprises. The main purpose of launching related sidelines is to capitalize on your company's name and reputation; this gives you a distinct advantage over competitors who must start from scratch.

4. Pick sidelines that can make good use of your existing employees. During slack periods in one business, the workers are kept busy in one of the other operations. Thus, Roy's men are active in the spring and early summer with pool installation and lawn-sprucing; during the rest of the year, they spend more of their time on the three home-improvement specialties he offers.

Picking related sidelines that make the most efficient use of your equipment and personnel, and cash in on your name and reputation, can truly do for you what it did for Roy—make your name worth a million dollars.

EXAMINE THESE SIDELINE EXAMPLES

If my publisher were to allow me the space contained in a 20-volume encyclopedia, I might be able to list all of the sideline possibilities that exist today. Since this isn't practical, I'll do the next best thing: provide you with a list of a few examples in the knowledge that this will spark your imagination and enable you to home in on the availabilities in whatever principal field you choose.

What I'm going to do is list three related businesses on each line. Any of these could be your principal business, and any of the others could be the sidelines that are developed later.

Advertising	Public relations	Employee relations
Antique sales	Restoring furniture	Estate appraisals
Answering service	Secretarial service	Addressing service
Art gallery	Art school	Art supplies
Employment agency	Temporary help service	Watchman service
Fire alarms	Fire extinguishers	Burglar alarms
Restaurant	Gift shop	Motel
Printing	Shopper newspaper	Regional magazine
Hair styling	Wigs	Hair implants
Industrial cleaning	Truck cleaning	Sandblasting
Insurance	Real estate	Business brokerage
Dog Kennel	Dog breeding	Pet supplies

As I say, the examples could go on and on, but you get the point. And there's another point of which you should be aware: One of your sidelines could out-produce, outgrow, and "out-profit" your initial venture. We'll look into that possibility next.

WHEN SIDELINES BECOME "MAINLINES"

I'll bet you didn't know these facts:

The giant Sears, Roebuck Company was started by a station agent in Redwood, Minnesota, whose only product was pocket watches that he sold to his fellow station agents.

Black and Decker, the famous maker of tools for home craftsmen, began by building adding machines and typesetters.

Heathkit, the firm that makes build-at-home electronic kits, got its start not in electronics, but by selling airplane kits.

Eastern Airlines made its first money not by carrying passengers, but by carrying the mail.

DuPont, known today as one of the world's largest producers of plastics, started out by manufacturing gunpowder.

Each of these firms, and thousands of other multi-million-dollar empires, found greater opportunities and larger profits in fields other than the one in which they began. Go back over the stories of today's self-made millionaires as related in earlier chapters of this book, and you'll find many similar experiences.

When I mention this point, people often ask me: "How, then, can I predict what is going to be my most profitable field?" The answer, of course, is that you can't. And there's an important lesson to be learned from all this:

Not until you've actually gone into business will you ever know what you missed!

If Richard Sears had not decided to sell watches, he never would have dreamed of creating America's leading mail order company. Had Ray Kroc not been in the business of selling food mixers, he probably would never have founded the giant McDonald's hamburger chain. If Howard Johnson had decided against operating a stationery and ice cream store, the huge restaurant and motel chain that bears his name would probably never have come into being.

That's why I urge you to put your going-into-business dream into action as soon as possible. I don't mean, naturally, that by starting the first business that comes to mind you will automatically be led into a series of million-dollar opportunities. I do mean that, by following the examples of the SMMs in this book, by making instant use of the hard-knocks knowledge it took them years to acquire, there's no telling how far you can go.

TECHNIQUES THAT CUT COSTS
AND MULTIPLY DOLLARS

As a person seriously interested in business, you recognize that there are two ways to increase profits. One way is, of course, to increase sales volume. And the other is to cut down on expenses. SMMs are not only aware of both methods, they constantly strive to practice them both.

In fact, cost-cutting is a prime concern in any business. But it has to be done in such a way that quality and efficiency are not hurt. SMMs have learned how to cut costs in a way that also increases profits. Sounds impossible? Read on.

One of the most successful practitioners of the art of cutting costs and increasing profits has been hotel magnate Conrad Hilton. Most of the Hilton hotels are located in areas of high real estate and tax costs. Nearly every inch of space has to be put to productive use.

In the Conrad Hilton Hotel in Chicago, for example, he built the profitable Williford Room by slicing another room in half. And because the ceiling was particularly high, he was able to create still another new room by installing a floor about half-way up. Elsewhere in Chicago, at the Palmer House, Hilton found that a bookshop was not returning much profit; so he replaced it with a cocktail lounge that increased the profit 200 times over.

At the Waldorf Astoria in Manhattan, Hilton's work crews took down two pillars that were serving no purpose and replaced them with showcases that brought in thousands of dollars in added income. Also in New York, at the Plaza, they converted storage space in the basement into a well-known wining and dining spot.

MULTIPLYING PROFITS BECOMES
A LIFELONG HABIT

The techniques outlined in this chapter have benefitted SMMs at the start of their careers and have remained with them constantly as their fortunes and empires grew.

Conrad Hilton was a multi-millionaire when he installed those new facilities in several of his hotels as mentioned above—but you can be sure that similar techniques earlier in his career helped him to become a multi-millionaire.

Similarly, the founders of the Wham-O Manufacturing Company (creators of the Hula Hoop and other innovative playthings) practiced cost-cutting, profit-increasing techniques right from the start. I've already told you (in an earlier chapter) how their first business enterprise was unrelated to toy manufacturing, and how they spotted toys as a highly profitable sideline activity and cashed in on it. Starting from scratch as they did, cost-cutting was a necessity. Their initial product—slingshots—was produced by the two partners themselves, and it was sold by them as well.

As additional products were added to the line and sales picked up, they moved to larger quarters and began adding employees. As many other businessmen have done, they found it practical to farm out part of their work. This can be an important cost-cutting technique because it allows you to have a flexible production capacity. Without subcontracting, you must have production facilities capable of handling your peak workloads. But what happens during temporary slack periods? A percentage of your facilities and your employees are idle, and this costs money.

THE FORTUNE-BUILDING COMBINATION

Here are three of the leading areas in which most SMMs make a habit of cutting costs and multiplying profits:

1. Space
2. Personnel
3. Advertising

Let's take a look at some examples of how successful businessmen increase their "cost-effectiveness" in these three areas.

CASH IN ON EXTRA SPACE

Unused space not only costs money, it means lost profits. That's why so many successful stores and even service agencies use this space to display extra products for customers to buy "on impulse." The customer walks into a shop with the idea of buying one particular product or service, spots the "impulse" displays, and winds up buying more than he or she bargained for.

A major American bus company has greatly increased its profits by using the luggage space located beneath the passenger compartment. It provides city-to-city parcel delivery—promising speed that the post office can't compete with.

The owner of a midwestern movie theater makes profitable use of his building's formerly idle morning hours. He rents the auditorium to a number of large corporations located nearby. They use it for sales meetings.

And when it comes time for growing corporations to build their own headquarters building, they often cut costs and increase profits by arranging to rent part of the space to other companies.

PERSONNEL POLICIES THAT PAY OFF

Making the most effective use (or even non-use) of personnel can mean added dollars in your corporate pocket.

When the nature of your business requires hiring personnel with specialized skills, there may be times when those skills are not needed for your day-to-day operations. That is, for example, the reason that a large New York radio station has some of its engineering employees also involved in a sideline business that sells and installs mobile communications equipment in taxis, police cars, and school buses.

Other businesses find it more efficient to hire employees on a "piecework" basis. A well-known foreign language school calls in its instructors only for periods when they are needed. It has no difficulty finding teachers willing to work on a part-time "call-in" basis, and it saves having to pay them full-time salaries.

As for effective "non-use" of personnel, many companies are finding added savings—and added profits—from the practical use of automated equipment run by computers. Even small offices are saving money these days by using mini-computers for record-keeping and billing, and by using automatic typewriters (known as word-processors) to handle the routine clerical tasks that formerly were performed by humans. Such equipment usually pays for itself within a year or two, and from then on it adds big pluses to the profit and loss statement.

PROFITS FROM ADVERTISING

For many businesses, advertising comprises a major expense, but a number of firms have figured out ways to have other companies share the expense. That's why mail order companies rent out their customer lists to other firms. It brings in extra dollars for very little effort.

You may have noticed that the bills you receive from the bank charge card companies almost always include "stuffer" brochures touting consumer products that you can order at the same time you pay your bill. The charge card company receives many additional dollars in profit from these sales.

Even such a large and prestigious mail order firm as Montgomery Ward has begun accepting outside advertising in its mail order catalog. Why would anybody want to advertise in somebody else's catalog? Simply because few other periodic publications are kept for so long or referred to so often.

BUILD A "FAMILY TREE" OF BUSINESSES

Perhaps you've seen your own family tree; if not, you probably have seen one compiled for another family; from one trunk sprout many branches. The holdings of many self-made millionaires can be likened to a family tree. One business—their initial one—was the progenitor of many other "offspring" enterprises, and together they comprise a family of businesses.

The story of James Ryder illustrates this point perfectly. He began after realizing that more money could be made working for himself in the trucking business than in his job of loading other peoples' trucks. And, after entering the trucking business, it came to him that providing trucks for other companies to use might be more profitable yet. So, he went into the truck leasing business. That was the trunk of his tree.

The branches? His business has spread out into such fields as car leasing and equipment rentals, the equipment covering a broad range of items including factory machines and office devices. Ryder System, Inc. also includes a large shipping company acquired along the way.

Jim Ryder, the man who began it all with a $30 investment (which went toward the purchase of his first truck) has been able to remove himself from the day-to-day operations of his empire. He has retired as chairman of the board, letting other people run things while he enjoys his $250,000 home and his yachts. He's also dabbling in some other investment interests, because few SMMs are ever able to divorce themselves completely from the fascinating field of business.

THE "RELATIVITY THEORY" IN BUSINESS

The mathematical genius, Einstein, was most noted for developing a theory of relativity in the field of physics. There is also a theory of relativity when it comes to building a business empire. And it's far easier to understand than the teachings of Einstein.

What is the business theory of relativity? Well, for one thing, you've seen it in action over and over again in the pages of this book. Simply put, it is this:

Most SMMs build their empires by creating or acquiring businesses in related fields.

Recall some of the empire-builders you've met so far. Howard Johnson developed a chain of restaurants; wasn't it a "natural" for him to build motels to go alongside those restaurants, and then to develop food lines bearing his famous name? William Lear was involved in creating innovative products, from the first car radio to the latest corporate jet. Richard Knerr went from slingshots to the Hula Hoop, to many other subsequent products. And Jim Ryder went from leasing trucks to leasing cars and typewriters.

Large, billion-dollar corporations can afford to diversify into a wide range of fields; in fact, they often have to do this because concentrating on any one industry can make you vulnerable to slides in the economy of that particular industry. But smaller firms that are on-the-grow gain their best growth by expanding in related fields. That's because you perform best at what you know best, and until you're big enough to have an active board of directors and high-paid executives, *you've* got to remain in the driver's seat doing what you do best.

EMPIRE-BUILDING SECRETS
OF THE MILLIONAIRES

A few years ago, I took a guided tour of major European countries. There were about 40 people on the tour, and I got to know a few of them quite well. One was a self-made multi-millionaire. On several occasions, following the day's sight-seeing, we had dinner together. During and after dinner, we had long talks about his highly successful career.

"I didn't get rich by doing anything anybody else couldn't have done," Ed H. told me. "My businesses all have been fairly common ones—the type anyone with an average set of brains could enter."

Naturally, I wanted to know what set him apart from other people—what turned his enterprises into million-dollar entities while other people in the same line of work struggled merely to eke out a living.

"Early on," he explained, "I learned that there are extra profits to be made from just about any business situation. Most people ignore these extra opportunities; I never have. These extra profits give you more capital with which to expand. So, while others stagnated, I grew."

"What kind of extra profits are you talking about?" I asked.

"Here's an example. My first venture into real estate, as a young man, was to buy a small apartment building in the city where I lived. It was six stories, fully rented, and making money. Most people would have been satisfied with this, but not I. So I converted the apartments on the first floor into professional offices, renting them to doctors and lawyers. I got nearly double the rental for those apartments.

And you know something? That taught me that if you look at a situation closely enough, there's almost always a practical way to have it bring in more money!"

FINDING WINDFALL PROFIT OPPORTUNITIES

I asked Ed to give me some more examples of how he found ways to make situations more profitable, and I took notes as he spoke. While you may not enter any of the same business fields, the methods of developing such windfall profit opportunities are similar. So you can use Ed's experience as a guide. Here are some of the things that he did:

He used the profit from the sale of that first apartment as the down payment on a larger building. With the structure came a plot of land located to the rear and serving no useful purpose. He built a swimming pool there for the use of his tenants. Then he increased rentals by 15 percent.

Detecting a shortage of apartments in his community, he bought a site and decided to build a high-rise. But, instead of hiring a contractor, he served as his own contractor, hiring sub-contractors to do various phases of the work, just as the principal contractor would have done, had there been one.

His growing knowledge of real estate led him to open a brokerage, earning commissions by selling other people's property for them. It also gave him an inside track on what properties were available, enabling him to grab some of the best pieces as soon as they were placed on the market.

Only a small percentage of the people who walk into a real estate office looking for something to buy actually end up buying through that office. Ed found a way to make money from many of those who entered his office, whether or not they became purchasers of real estate. How? By installing a shelf of practical books on real estate subjects—how to find the right home, etc. Penny-ante, you say? Earning $20 to $30 in extra profit each day for very little additional effort is not to be sneezed at.

Ed's success with that book-shelf sideline prompted him to take over a store that had become vacant in one of the shopping centers that he owned. He set up the store as a bookshop containing only "how-to" books. Knowing that Americans are great "do-it-yourselfers," he realized that there is a great market for books telling them how to do it. No matter what your hobby or spare-time interest, you'll find instructional volumes on the subject in that store.

The how-to bookstore was such a success that Ed soon recognized that there was a market for such books not only in his own community, but across the country. So he opened up a mail order division, advertising in many of the handyman and handicraft magazines.

Ed H., as you can see, is quite an entrepreneur. And I've given you only a few examples of the windfall profit opportunities he related to me during our series of conversations.

The point to be learned from the examples I have given is this:

In practically any money-making situation, there is an oppor-

tunity to make even more money. It doesn't take a stroke of
genius; all it takes is the ability to spot the opportunity.

How do you develop such an ability? That's what we'll be
discussing next.

LEARN HOW TO SPOT
WINDFALL OPPORTUNITIES

Let's assume you've started your first business. Your empire-
building process is finally underway. And what's more, your enterprise is making money—fairly good money. But, if you're doing
only as well as anybody else might do in the same type of business,
there is no reason to sit back and congratulate yourself. You're not
doing well enough.

For the fact is this: If you're only doing as well as your average
competitor, you have failed to cash in on the windfall opportunities
that are open to you! Any business can make extra profits by utilizing one or more of these techniques:

- Incidental sale of related products or services
- Upgrading the average sale
- Having others share your items of heavy cost

Actually, you've seen these techniques in action in the case
histories and other examples given so far in this chapter. But, to
make sure they are absolutely clear to you—so you'll be ready to
profit from them when the time comes—let's take a closer look at
each of the techniques.

SELL INCIDENTAL PRODUCTS OR SERVICES

This is the easiest of the three techniques to employ, and the
one most often overlooked by beginning businessmen. It's based
on the "impulse-buying" theory employed by so many department
stores. They know that people enter the store with only one or two
purchases in mind, but frequently act on impulse and buy other
items that they have spotted on display.

Sometimes the "impulse" purchase can be much larger than
the main one. A couple in Vermont has made many, many
thousands of dollars this way. They operate a country inn with half
a dozen rooms rented out by the night to tourists, hunters, and

skiers visiting their area. They converted their extra-large home into an inn merely to help meet the tax and utility bills. One day, it dawned on them that many visitors to Vermont are prime prospects to buy vacation land there. So they went into the real estate brokerage business.

On the dresser in each room they rent is a mimeographed listing of their currently-listed property. This, together with informal conversations with the guests as they are signing the register or checking out, has led to many sales. In fact, the couple has an advantage over all other brokers in the area; they get "first crack" at some of the best prospective property buyers to visit the region.

The lesson to be learned is this: Whether your business sells products or services, more money can be made by offering additional products and services to the same people. Sometimes the "incidental" part of your business can grow to become its prime source of profit.

UPGRADE YOUR AVERAGE SALE

Let's assume that your business averages about 10 percent profit on gross sales. And maybe you're already operating to the hilt; you can't increase sales without enlarging your place of business and adding on more employees. Not being ready to make such an additional investment, is there then no way in which you can increase profits?

There is a very logical way. It involves upgrading your average sale. This means, simply, that you sell higher-priced items. Thus, you take in more money for the same amount of effort, and because you earn ten cents in profit on the dollar, your profits climb accordingly.

Smart businessmen are finding practical ways to do this every day. Some examples:

- The insurance broker who switches from private accounts to industrial accounts
- The accountant who gives up preparing income tax returns in favor of doing accounting work for businesses in his or her community
- The boat dealer who upgrades his inventory from small trailerable craft to take in larger, more expensive boats.

- The lawnmower repair shop that decides to take on the higher-paying repairs of outboard engines
- The door-to-door salesman who finds that selling vacuum cleaners can be a lot more profitable than selling perfume or brushes
- The manufacturer of small computers who begins making computer kits for hobbyists and then decides to earn thousands, instead of hundreds, of dollars per sale by selling computers to small business firms

These are just a few of thousands of examples that I could give you, but I'm sure you get the point by now. Upgrading the level-of-sale is one of the most powerful techniques for enlarging your base of profits. All kinds of companies do it—from the very smallest to the very largest. In fact, many firms that get into their line of business at "the low end of the market" move as soon as they can into the higher categories.

SHARE ITEMS OF HEAVY COST

You learned earlier in this chapter that cost-cutting can be as effective as increasing sales when it comes to boosting profits. Suppose you sell something for $20, and it costs $15 to produce. To increase your $5 profit to $8, you can either increase the price you charge to $23, or reduce its cost-to-you to $12. Or you can split it up by cutting the cost $1.50 and boosting the price $1.50.

If you're faced with a lot of competition, though, increasing the price just may not be practical. So you have to find a way to cut costs while maintaining quality. The way many forward-thinking businessmen have accomplished this is to pick one or more of their biggest expense items and have others share the cost.

I can hear you saying it now. "How in the world can I get other people to share my expenses?" It's being done every day. Here are just a few of the methods:

- Professional men and women, such as doctors and lawyers, often share office space.
- Because their presses are idle much of the time, many newspaper publishers take on outside printing work— usually for other newspapers.

- Owners of shopping malls help meet their operating expenses by renting booth space in their lobbies, or using the lobbies for trade shows (cars and boats are two examples) at which exhibitors pay rental fees.
- The owners of drive-in theaters rent out their property on Saturdays and Sundays for flea markets.
- The proprietors of many businesses frequented by the public allow vending machine operators to install their machines on the premises, receiving a cut of the profits; the only expense to the proprietor is for the small amount of space and electricity required by the machine.

Think a bit and you can add many items to the list yourself, just from what you have personally observed in the business world. The moral of it all is this:

Expenses can be shared by having other business firms pay for making use of some valuable commodity that your business possesses but doesn't need to use all the time.

WINDFALL BY WINDFALL, YOU CAN BECOME RICH

Some of the profit-boosting, cost-cutting methods related in this chapter may seem minor when compared to your million-dollar goals. Increasing profits by a few percentage-points won't in itself convert a small businessman into a millionaire, but it does make the going a lot easier. And remember this: The person who is cost-conscious and profit-alert from the outset will benefit throughout his or her career. It may mean only a few hundred or a few thousand dollars now, but the same type of tactic will mean hundreds of thousands and even millions of dollars when you reach the SMM category.

And now that you've received a good grounding in the way SMMs deal with costs and profits, let's turn to the much more spectacular methods they use for multiplying their financial holdings with great speed. Millionaires are usually not made overnight—but often in a year or so, and the next chapter tells you how.

12

How to Make Your Profits Snowball

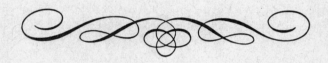

You are about to learn some of the more spectacular techniques that make multi-millionaires out of common folk such as you and me. The methods are spectacular because they can convert a person of ordinary financial means into a man or woman of fabulous wealth in a surprisingly short period of time. And yet these methods are simple.

Spectacular? Simple? How can a wealth-building method be both?

It is spectacular, because of the huge gain in financial worth that is achieved. It is simple, because each of the techniques follows a formula that has been employed by thousands of self-made millionaires. And the formulas work regardless of your type of business; it can be in retailing, electronics, real estate, business services, entertainment, health care—you name it.

Here are the four formulas you'll learn in this chapter:

1. The Branch Profits Formula
2. The Franchising Formula
3. The Stock Sale Formula
4. The Merger Formula

You can easily handle the first formula on your own. And when the time comes to explore the succeeding three formulas, you'll have experts at your command to guide you all the way.

So let's get started!

USE THE BRANCH PROFITS FORMULA

You were introduced to the theory behind the Branch Profits Formula early in this book. It's based on what I call the Success Repetition Factor. Simply put, it is this: Once you have established a money-making business, repeat your success over and over again by using the exact same methods to open up similar businesses elsewhere. But how, precisely, do you go about doing it? The Branch Profits Formula tells how.

Here are the basic steps in the Formula:

1. Launch your "pilot" business close to home so you can personally guide it into a profit-making status.
2. As you operate the business, work out the "bugs" so that it is a smoothly-operating, self-sufficient enterprise.
3. When it has reached the point of bringing in a steady flow of profits, use those profits to open up a branch elsewhere, using your proven operating methods.
4. When the second business is firmly established (and this will happen more rapidly than the first time around because of the experience you have gained) use the combined profits of the first two businesses to open up a third branch.
5. As the number of your branches grows, the mounting combination of profits allows you to open additional branches with even greater speed. At this point, you can be planning several new branches simultaneously instead of just one at a time.
6. Build your empire until the number of branches brings you the level of profits you desire. At this point, you might wish to multiply your net worth by using one of the other formulas in this chapter.

THE MAGIC OF THE
BRANCH PROFITS FORMULA

You have a very powerful factor going for you when you utilize the Branch Profits Formula:

All it takes to put the Formula in action is one successful business.

If you can do it once, you can do it a dozen times; or a hundred; or more. If you can launch just one successful small business, you can do it repeatedly, multiplying your earnings with each additional outlet you open. This way, a "small" business becomes big business—with a capital "B"!

THE QUESTION THEY ALL ASK

When I explain the Branch Profits Formulas to them, most people just starting out on the SMM road can readily understand its power and effectiveness. But every last one of them asks me a question that goes something like this: "How could I possibly manage ten—or even three—stores or offices? When would I ever get any sleep?"

The answer is that once you start the expansion process, you cease managing any of your branches at all, not even the original outlet that got the ball rolling.

Think about it for a minute. The last time you entered a McDonald's restaurant, did you see Ray Kroc behind the counter? And when you visit a Sears store, is the chairman of the board anywhere to be seen? Of course not. Each of these giant companies—and each of the many other firms that operate branches—have branch managers to run things for them.

Here's how it works. As you develop your initial business outlet, you train your top employee to manage its day-to-day operations. When the time comes to open a branch, he or she moves on to that branch as its manager. The best-performing employees of your first two outlets are then "brought along" in management training so they, too, can be moved into branch management slots as additional branches are opened.

Many companies also develop an Operations Manual to guide

each branch manager in the day-to-day operations of his store, office, or plant. This is to guarantee that the same techniques that spelled success for the initial branch are adhered to in succeeding branches.

THE BRANCH PROFITS FORMULA IN ACTION

Winston Schuler, the millionaire restaurateur you've already met in this book, started with one little eatery situated in a small hotel in Michigan. In building his empire to the point where he is now worth well over $10,000,000 he has repeated his initial success many times. And although he (and now his son) visit the newer restaurants from time to time, they depend on local managers to keep things going.

Schuler opened one of his first branches because he wanted to prove that someone else could run a business following the precise formula that he had created. It worked, and as Schuler gained confidence in additional promising employees, he opened additional restaurants.

HOW TO GO NATIONAL OR EVEN WORLDWIDE

Walk into just about any American town and you'll see scores of successful, profitable businesses. Walk into a neighboring town and you'll see similar business establishments, selling the same products and services, and earning equivalent profits.

Most of these businesses are owned by the individuals who run them, and each of the proprietors usually has just the one business. This is fine for spreading the wealth, but have you ever wondered why an individual who owns a successful business in Town A couldn't run a similar establishment in Town B—and maybe Towns C and D as well? Spreading the wealth is fine, but I assume that the reason you're reading this book is that you want to concentrate some of the wealth right in your own bank account.

So don't be a "small-minded" businessman. Open your initial business in Town A, certainly. But have as your early goal the establishment of branches in other communities as well.

And do you know something? You don't have to confine your operations to the United States. There are particular advantages to having your empire become global in nature. Read on.

BROADEN YOUR SCOPE
FOR BROADER OPPORTUNITIES

There are those who complain that the day of the SMM in America is nearly over. They gripe that taxes, government regulations, consumerism, the energy shortage, and a dozen other factors are making it too difficult to build a fortune anymore. Well, that's just not the case, as you've seen in the pages of this book. New fortunes are being made practically every day—and will continue to be made.

But it is true that earning a million dollars is a little more complex than it used to be. Growing bureaucracy, etc., has made that inevitable. Do I hear you saying, "Ah, for the good old days?" My friend, the good old days exist right now. Not here, but right now. Allow me to explain.

THE RETURN OF THE GOOD OLD DAYS

If you think it would have been far easier to earn a fortune in America a few decades ago, or perhaps even a half or full century ago, stop pining and get moving—to another part of the world. For the fact is that many other nations on this globe of ours are at the same point of development that the U.S. was years and years ago.

What's in this for you? For one thing, it means that a business plan that may be old hat here in the United States hasn't even been explored yet in many foreign lands. And we all know that the first person with a good business idea is likely to make a financial killing.

Simple everyday businesses that would be highly competitive here in America provide outstanding opportunities abroad. You might, for example, hesitate to open a laundromat in your home town because there are already too many laundromats. And so how can you put our Branch Profits Formula in motion if it's too risky even to get your first store open and in business? You've already guessed the answer. You do it overseas. People in many underdeveloped countries have never even heard of laundromats, let alone seen one. Imagine what kind of opportunity this presents!

Whether you want to start your enterprise in Mexico, South

America, Africa, the Middle East, or in some European nation depends on two things:

(1) Your own personal preference of locale
(2) The opportunities and problems existing in a given country.

In other words, you shouldn't plan on opening up your chain of laundromats in just any old country. For one thing, you might not like living in that country. And for another, the country might not look favorably on the type of business you have in mind.

The procedure to follow, then, is to (1) pick the country where you'd like to live and work, (2) choose a product or service you can provide that is in short supply there, and (3) check out whatever governmental complications might exist in that land.

It has been done many times by many Americans, among them Frank C., who introduced the idea of a car rental agency in a major city in a friendly South American nation. It's old hat here in the U.S., true, but rare in the country Frank zeroed in on. His first car rental agency was so successful that Frank has opened branches in several other cities. Even before he was a millionaire in that nation's currency, he was living better than most American millionaires, thanks to the lower cost of luxury in his adopted land.

So if you've got an idea for a little business you'd enjoy starting, consider opening it in some foreign land of your liking. You just may find that your "little" business becomes big a lot faster.

USE THE FRANCHISING FORMULA

As we move on to the second formula in our series, a definition is in order. The term franchising does not mean buying a franchise for, say, a hotdog stand. It means selling franchises—many of them—for a proven business plan you have developed. There's a lot more money to be made being a franchisor than being a franchisee.

Look in the Business Opportunities column of your newspaper's classified section and you'll probably see dozens of ads inserted by companies having franchises to sell. Many people don't know it, but most of these companies started on a very small scale—often as a "mom and pop" type store. The business techniques they developed worked so well, they decided to open branches. And they found that letting other people pay to open and run branches for you can be a lot easier and a lot more profitable than doing it yourself.

Here's what the Franchising Formula consists of:

1. Pick a field (generally retail or service) and open a "pilot" store, office, or agency. Develop it to the point where it is profitable and can be operated by a hired manager.

2. Open one or more branches at other locations, testing out the business techniques you have developed at the first location.

3. When you have demonstrated that the operating techniques are equally workable at different locations, put together a franchise "package." You can handle this yourself, or you can retain the services of a company that specializes in packaging franchise deals. The package involves training franchisees to operate branch establishments of your business. In return for the franchise fee that they pay you, you provide the proven operating method plus help in picking a business location and obtaining the needed equipment and supplies.

4. You continue to earn money from each franchised location because of (1) royalties you charge based on gross sales, (2) profit you make on selling supplies to the franchisees, or both.

5. When the number of franchised outlets warrants, consider selling stock in your corporation for an almost instantaneous boost in your net worth. (See the Stock Sale Formula to be outlined a bit later in this chapter.)

This Franchising Formula, with slight variations, has been used with spectacular success by many of today's best-known franchisors. Among them: Ray Kroc of McDonald's, Harland Sanders and his successors at Kentucky Fried Chicken, Kemmons Wilson of Holiday Inns, Howard Johnson of the restaurant and motel chain that bears his name, Jean Nidetch of Weight Watchers, and hundreds of others whose names might not be as familiar to you.

THE ADVANTAGES OF FRANCHISING

"Why," you may ask, "should I share my business system with somebody else when I can open branches on my own and keep all the profit?" There are a number of important reasons to consider franchising. Examine these factors:

1. The investment capital required for opening each branch is put up by the franchisee who opens that branch. It's usually a combination of his own cash and financing that has been arranged for him. Thus your chain can grow much more rapidly, since you are not depending on your own capital for expansion purposes.

2. The risk is largely that of the franchisee, not the franchisor. Naturally, you stand to lose something if the branch fails—but most of the risk is borne by the owner of that branch.

3. People with an equity in a business will work harder toward the success of that business than will those who are merely hired hands. Thus you can expect a lot more from a franchisee than from a hired manager.

4. Because each branch is locally owned, it gains better acceptance in and by the local community. Customers like doing business at locally-owned establishments.

5. Your operating, advertising, and personnel costs are much lower than they would be if you continued to operate each branch on your own. This is because you now devote your efforts merely to obtaining and supervising franchisees rather than operating scores of businesses on a day-to-day basis.

6. You enjoy the benefits of financial leverage and people leverage. You have going for you the money sent you by each franchisee and the labor he and his employees put forth. Your empire, therefore, is built largely with outside money and labor.

Setting up a franchise offering can be easier than you think. In fact, when you're ready it can be done for you. A number of companies specialize in handling just such deals. Look for their ads in such business publications as the Wall Street Journal, or contact your nearest office of the Small Business Administration. An SBA specialist should be able to steer you to a franchise-packager located in your part of the country.

SPECTACULAR SUCCESS IN FRANCHISING

A 31-year-old Californian named Al Lapin got an idea for a pancake house in Burbank. He signed up a couple of relatives and three other silent partners, putting together a total investment of $25,000 for the first International House of Pancakes.

The success of the first restaurant led to other branches, to franchising, and to stock sales, as Lapin adhered pretty much to the Franchising Formula. In fact, his success with the pancake restaurant business prompted him to launch franchises in other fields as well.

Al Lapin, and all others who have successfully branched out into additional fields, have proven this fact:

The secret in franchising is not selling pancakes, office services, or automobile repairs—it is in renting a proven system of doing business.

Pay particular heed to the phrase "renting a proven system." In franchising you aren't really selling anything. Oh, the contract may say that you sell the franchisee the right to deal in your product or service, but it's actually a rental because he must continue making payments to you throughout the period of the contract.

Al Lapin is living proof that the method can be spectacularly successful. That first little restaurant has led to an empire with franchise packages in over a dozen different fields, and with a financial worth of well over a hundred million dollars.

USE THE STOCK SALE FORMULA

When the average small businessman thinks of selling stock, the only thing he has in mind is raising capital with which to expand his business. But when the budding SMM thinks of selling stock, he has something far more breathtaking in mind.

The motive of the future SMM is not merely to expand his business, but also to expand his own net worth—almost instantly.

Let's see how it works.

1. Let's say a budding millionaire sets up a small manufacturing operation in some currently glamorous field, perhaps making micro-computers for small businesses. (Many people have started such businesses on a shoestring.) His initial investment is $10,000, augmented by borrowed cash.

2. After a year or two, earnings reach $2-million. The budding millionaire decides it's time for a stock offering. He hires an attorney and an accountant to set up the deal. Stock speculators like his company's performance. They buy up 45 percent of his firm's stock, paying about seven times earnings (a conservative figure).

3. Seven times the company's earnings of $2-million means the firm is valued at $14-million. This means that our budding millionaire is no longer a budding millionaire. He is a real one. Remember, he owns 55 percent of the stock; 55 percent of $14-million is $7.7-million, and that's how much our friend is now worth.

4. In addition to being worth $7.7-million dollars, our friend has received a windfall of $6.3-million in cash from the stock sale proceeds. This is not his own money to keep, of course; it goes into the company's treasury. But it doesn't just sit there. Mr. Millionaire uses it to expand his business, developing a new line of computers.

5. With the new line of products, sales volume more than doubles in a very short time. Wall Street is really beginning to sit up and take notice. Now the analysts value the stock at ten times earnings, figuring that a company with such spectacular growth has to be really going places. Ten times the earnings of $4-milllion is $40-million. Our friend's stake in this is 55 percent of $40-million, or $22-million. Not bad for a $10,000 investment!

6. Losing interest in the business he developed, our friend decides to sell out. He can either place his own stock on the market and reap the $22-million in capital gains, or he can sell his firm to a larger computer company, taking

stock in the well-established firm as his payment, and earning gigantic dividends for the rest of his life.

7. Or, he could do something with even bigger stakes in mind. He could use the equity of his smallish company to take control of a much larger firm. Playing his cards right, within a short period he could be worth hundreds of millions of dollars instead of a measly $22-million.

Does it sound too stupendous to be possible? It's been done many, many times, and it's still being done today. As you read on, you'll learn how others have done it and how you can, too.

MULTIPLY YOUR NET WORTH THROUGH STOCK SALES

In the last chapter, you learned how Jean Nidetch used the sale of related products to enhance her Weight Watchers fortune. But that's far from all she's done. Stock sales have enhanced her fortune even more.

When Mrs. Nidetch and her partners decided to "go public" (offer some of their stock to the public) the price-per-share jumped from $11.25 to $40 in just one day. This means that at the close of business that day, the Weight Watchers entrepreneurs were worth almost four times what they were when the business day began.

How does one "go public?" There are two ways; you can do it yourself, or you can retain the services of a professional underwriter. Most SMMs who have gone the "public" route recommend the latter method. Why? Simply because professional underwriters can handle it for you at less trouble and expense than if you were to try it yourself.

A study by the Federal Reserve Bank of Boston revealed that more than twice as many stock-issues handled by professional underwriters have been successful as those that are handled by the businessman himself.

And how does one locate a professional underwriter? By the time you've reached the point where you're even considering this, you will have become friendly with a number of bankers. Any one of your acquaintances in the banking community can aim you in the direction of the nearest underwriter's office.

USE THE MERGER METHOD
FOR VASTLY INCREASED WEALTH

Step 7 of the Stock Sale Formula presented an idea that may have fascinated you if you are true SMM material. It told of the possibility of using your smallish corporation's assets to take control of a much larger company. This, too, has been done many times.

Let's revisit two old friends from earlier chapters in this book—Jim Ryder and Meshulam Riklis. Our visit to Jim Ryder, founder of the Ryder System (trucking and car leasing, etc.), comes on that hectic day when his company took over a major trucking concern he'd had his heart set on acquiring.

Even after scraping together all of his company's funds and obtaining some loans, Ryder could come up with only half the amount needed to take over Great Southern Trucking Company. So what did he do? He used some of Great Southern's own assets as the balance of the purchase price. He worked out an arrangement to sell one of its large warehouses and used the cash proceeds toward his purchase price for the company.

I can sense that you have two questions. First, how could he sell a warehouse he didn't yet own? Well, it all happened within minutes, with a transfer of papers back and forth across the bargaining table. Naturally, the arrangements had been worked out in advance. Great Southern's sellers knew, and had agreed to, the warehouse deal. They got their cash, and that's all that really mattered.

Second question: How could he operate his newly-acquired company without that all-important warehouse? Answer: He couldn't and he didn't. Part of the deal was that he would lease it back from the new owner, paying the rental fees out of continuing income.

Leasing, as you learned back in Chapter 3, is a powerful means of raising needed cash. It spares you from having to lay out a big sum for property or equipment you need for the operation of your business. And, as in Ryder's case, it can help you buy a business.

Our visit with Meshulam Riklis could occur almost any day. He has been involved in so many corporate acquisitions since leaving his low-paying office job that you could almost throw a dart at the calendar and on that day you'd find him negotiating a new deal. But let's look at one of his first deals, because it demonstrates that you don't have to buy an entire company to gain the benefit of its assets and its profits. All you have to do is buy enough stock to gain control of the company. And when a corporation has many different stockholders, substantially less than 50 percent of the stock will give you effective control.

On the first day that we visit Riklis, he has put up cash equivalent to just one-seventh of the total assets of Rapid Electrotype Company. We pay a return visit not long afterwards, and discover that Riklis, now the chief executive officer of Rapid Electrotype, is using that firm's cash and assets to acquire still other companies. And we could return again and again and see the same type of thing happening. After all, that's how his multi-billion dollar empire was built.

USE THE MERGER FORMULA FOR VASTLY INCREASED WEALTH

Now that you've seen the Merger Formula in action let's spell out the rules. Here they are:

1. Build up your company to the point where it can go public, and then do it.

2. Use the proceeds of the stock sale to expand your company's operations, thereby increasing its sales.

3. Having an increased value, your company is now in the position of making acquisitions. Look for larger firms whose stock is widely held, meaning that a small percentage of the other company's stock can give you effective operating control.

4. Use some of the stock in your own firm as the financing with which you acquire control of the other company.

5. After gaining control of the second firm, use its substantially greater assets to continue the acquisition process.

The wonderful thing about the Merger Formula is that once your initial company is formed and made profitable, little or no cash is required to carry on the building of your empire. The "money" that changes hands is all on paper. Stock is traded for stock, using leverage to the hilt. A little stock buys a lot more stock in a different company.

"They're talking about the cashless society," a prominent SMM recently told me, "but I'm already living in it. To the general public, 'cashless society' means the use of credit cards and the like, but to me it means using stock and other forms of leverage to build my holdings."

Does he ever get to see any cash? "Sure I do. As the chairman of several boards, I take home more than $300,000 per year in salaries. Then there are dividends on all the stock I own. And now that I've achieved most of my financial goals in life, I'm beginning to sell some of my stock holdings. So there's a tremendous amount of cash in-flow here."

What's he going to do with all that cash? "Probably buy more stock—only this time in corporations I'm not involved in. Let others go to the office every day; I'm going to sit back and count my blessings!"

Thanks to the Merger Formula, his blessings are many.

A BIG DAY IS COMING—
SOONER THAN YOU THINK

The astonishing strides that you can make by opening branches, going into franchising, going public, and merging with other companies, need not be far off. Some of these methods may seem awfully sophisticated to you right now, and they are indeed sophisticated. But as thousands of SMMs have proved, they are realistic and achievable. And you don't have to wait half a lifetime to do it.

Some of the most spectacular success stories related in this book occurred very rapidly. Remember, all it takes is one successful little business to get you started. Once your business system has been perfected, you're ready to "take it on the road." That means you're ready to repeat it over and over again in branch outlets, or to rent the system to franchisees, or to sell stock in the system to the investing public, or even to use the cash value of that system to buy into other people's systems.

How long does it take? Jean Nidetch quadrupled her financial holdings in Weight Watchers within the time span of one day. Jim Ryder took over a much larger company after only a few months of intensive negotiating. Meshulam Riklis has always moved rapidly from one company to another. So you don't have to wait until you're elderly and doddering before becoming a multi-millionaire. You can become one in less time than it takes to grow a few gray hairs.

KNOW THE POSSIBILITIES BEFORE YOU START

In this book we've come a long way. We began with a dream—your dream of somehow getting rich—and we have learned how you can convert that dream into a highly profitable business. We've outlined how that beginning business can be enlarged to the million-dollar category, and now we've been discussing how your empire can obtain truly vast holdings.

You may wonder why a book that tells you how to start your very first business also goes into complex matters as stock sales and mergers in such detail. After all, if you haven't opened the door to your first business, you're hardly ready to acquire someone else's multi-million dollar corporation.

Well, the fact is that even before you hang out your very first shingle, you should have a general idea of where you are going—that is if you truly want some day soon to be counted in the SMM category. Know now the possibilities open to you and you can gear the growth of your enterprise accordingly. And by now you should recognize the two key steps involved in building a multi-million-dollar empire:

1. Build a proven business operating system.
2. Use the financial value of that system as leverage in applying any of the four formulas outlined in this chapter.

Step One is the proving ground. Step Two is where the really big money is made. Once you have a proven business operating system, you have something others are clamoring for. It can reap tremendous dividends, worth far more than the money and effort you devoted to developing it.

PUT YOUR MONEY TO WORK FOR YOU

Having a fortune of your own will mean a lot more to you than merely allowing you to buy a lot of material things you've always wanted. Ask any SMM, as I have, and you'll learn that they didn't become millionaires merely to be able to buy a jet plane or a European castle. Most of them did it for:

(1) The challenge

(2) The pride of achievement

(3) The prestige and power it gives them

(4) The ability to help others

(5) The improved lifestyle

Yes, money is important. But not only for the obvious reasons. That's why in the next chapter we'll let some of today's SMMs show us how to make the most of newfound wealth.

13

How to Keep Your Fortune and Enjoy Your Wealth

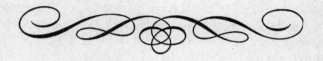

Most self-made millionaires will tell you that making the money is three-quarters of the fun. Naturally, there's a lot of pleasure to be had from the financial fruits of your labor, and I've never heard an SMM complain about the huge amount of money he's earned. But the fact is that most SMMs speak more of the pleasures of becoming rich than they do of the pleasures of being rich.

Not all of them, I fear, have learned how to get the most out of their newfound wealth. But, fortunately, many have, and it is from the experiences of these that the information in this chapter is drawn. For, just as much as I want you to become an SMM yourself, I want you to reap all the benefits of achieving that status.

And the first thing you've got to learn is how to keep as much money as you can, despite Uncle Sam's incessant efforts to wrest it away from you.

LEGAL TAX-BREAKS
THAT ARE YOURS FOR THE TAKING

Everyone, SMMs included, should want to pay his or her fair share of income taxes; but, why should you have to pay much more

than your share as a "reward" for breaking from the pack, showing
initiative, and developing a top money-making system? Look, the
purpose of this book is not to have you earn more money to turn
over to the Washington bureaucrats so they can spend it on additional giveaway programs. No, the purpose is to make more money
for *you*, and I wouldn't be doing my job if I didn't tell of the
effective methods used by SMMs to hold on to a goodly portion of
what is rightfully theirs.

From the start of their careers, SMMs have been especially
conscious of tax angles. They've had to be, or they wouldn't have
become SMMs. The graduated tax system forces those in the upper
income brackets to turn over the majority of their earnings to the
government.

And, so, what SMMs have done is to remove themselves from
the upper brackets. There are many legal ways of doing this, including:

- Depreciating property and equipment
- Extensive use of tax shelters
- Timing capital losses to offset gains
- Investing in tax-free municipal bonds
- Utilizing government-approved tax incentives

Entire encyclopedias have been written about tax strategy,
and, in fact, the manual for Internal Revenue Service agents has an
index that runs to a thousand pages—and that's just the index.
Thus, the best advice I can give you about taxes is to do what
virtually all SMMs have done, and that is to use the service of a tax
expert.

The way you go about setting up a business, how you log your
earnings, and what you do with them will have an important effect
on the amount of taxes you pay. This is true even in the very first
business you open, small as it may be. That's why you'll need to
contact an accountant as soon as your plans to set up shop have
been made final.

And, as your empire starts to grow, upgrade the level of tax
advice that you obtain. The bigger you are, the bigger the expert
you should consult. When you're in the million-dollar category, the
accountant located in a cubby hole upstairs over the drugstore just
won't suffice any longer.

But don't fall into the trap of fretting so much about taxes that you fail to push ahead with your business goals. A good accountant or tax attorney will handle all the details for you, and save you a lot more money than you will have to shell out in the way of fees.

HOW TO USE YOUR EXCESS CASH

As you follow in the footsteps of the SMMs you've read about in this book, sooner or later you're going to have a problem. A very pleasant problem, but nevertheless a problem. What do you do with all that money that's rolling in?

By now I'm sure you realize that being a millionaire or even a multi-millionaire does not mean that you have anything like a million dollars in readily available cash. Self-made millionaires—those who have not inherited huge fortunes—have most of their holdings tied up in their businesses and in their investments.

But with millions of dollars successfully invested, your personal cash flow is naturally going to be considerably more than if you were still, say, a clerk laboring at the local bank. So what do you do with it? As has been our habit throughout this book, we again turn to SMMs for guidelines.

As might be expected, some SMMs have had a difficult time adjusting to their newfound wealth. Just as they went through a "learning process" in developing their fortunes, they've had to go through a learning process in dealing with those fortunes. Since the purpose of this book is to give you the benefit of what took SMMs many years to learn, we'll examine the successful uses they've made of their money. With these as a guide, you can largely skip the trial-and-error process.

Here's what the majority of SMMs do with their cash after the needs of their businesses and families are met:

- Make personal investments that are not related to their businesses
- Help to underwrite worthwhile causes
- Pay for enhanced personal lifestyles
- Utilize money-power to give them positions of authority and respect in the community

These, then, are some of the wealth-uses we'll be discussing in this chapter. You'll see that you have a lot to look forward to.

MAKING PERSONAL INVESTMENTS FOR FUN AND PROFIT

One of the nicest advantages of being independently wealthy is that you can "dabble" in such things as:

- Art
- Antiques
- Thoroughbred horses
- The stock market

A lot of SMMs have gained twofold benefits from their spare-time interests in such fields. First, it provides a pleasant break from their workaday chores. And second, it helps diversify their financial holdings—spreading out the risk, so to speak. Let's take a closer look at each of these non-business-related investments.

Invest in Art: J. Paul Getty, frequently described as the world's richest billionaire, was an avid art collector. Naturally, he enjoyed it immensely. But he also realized that "buying fine art can be the finest and most satisfying of all investments." With his worldwide business holdings, Getty hardly needed art to boost his income or net worth, yet he proudly said that the value of many of his art possessions multiplied tremendously during the period that he owned them. And he noted that you can begin investing in fine art at any financial stage in your life, starting with only a few hundred dollars. It's a great investment habit to get into.

Collect Antiques: "Ever since I moved into my first apartment," says SMM Marcia B., "I've furnished my living quarters with antiques. First, of course, I love them—but even more important is the fact that, unlike new furniture that depreciates in value the moment you take it out of the store, antiques grow in value year by year." Marcia made her money in advertising, and now that she has a lot more of it, the quality of her antiques has risen accordingly. "The stock market may fluctuate widely," Marcia asserts, "but the value of my antiques never ceases to grow." Marcia enjoys traveling the world searching for and finding new "treasures" for her collection.

Raise Thoroughbred Horses: They call horse racing the sport of kings. Perhaps so, but buying, selling, and raising the animals used in this sport is a fascinating investment pursuit shared by many SMMs of non-royal blood. "People from all walks of life get involved in horse racing," comments Steve P., who made his millions in real estate, "and unfortunately, poor people get into the wrong end of the game—betting. There's just no way to win consistently at the track. But there is a way to win, and win handsomely, at the stable—by racing your own horses." The moral: stay away from the track while building your self-made fortune, but consider owning race horses as a pleasurable and profitable pursuit once your fortune is safely in hand.

Invest in Stocks: By far the most common investment among SMMs is stocks and bonds. That's because, either on their own or with the aid of an investment advisor, they can put their money in a broad range of securities, providing the maximum in diversity and safety. Some SMMs, such as mail order tycoon Hank L., maintain two types of portfolios. "One for conservative investments," Hank explains, "and the other to allow me to 'play around' a bit. I have more cash than I'll ever need, and one of the pleasures I have in life (outside my business) is putting money in highly speculative issues and watching what happens to it." How has he done? His conservative portfolio has shown a moderate, but steady, increase in value. "I've just about broken even on my speculative endeavors," Hank admits.

Naturally, there are many other fascinating—even exciting—ways you can utilize your excess cash for both enjoyment and growth. You might consider: rare coins, antique automobiles, absentee management real estate, owning an athletic team, underwriting Broadway shows, film producing, or even owning a TV station or two.

There are two criteria that most SMMs follow in making their spare-time investments:

1. To provide a change of pace, the investments should not be in the same field as your principal money-making endeavors.
2. The "dabbling" should be fun as well as profitable. If your sole purpose is to make money, you're probably better off turning your spare cash over to an investment advisor in a discretionary account, meaning the advisor has authority to make all the investment decisions for you.

HELP TO UNDERWRITE WORTHWHILE CAUSES

One of the biggest surprises in becoming rich is the unexpected joy you gain in being able to help others. It is indeed a surprise to many of the newly-rich, because their initial goal was to help themselves and their families—not other people. But once they start using some of their money for totally unselfed purposes, they experience a thrill they never expected.

Perhaps educator William Lyon Phelps put it best. Speaking of American millionaires, he said:

"As I travel about and see the results of their generosity in the form of hospitals, churches, public libraries, universities, parks, recreation grounds, art museums and theatres I wonder what on earth we should do without them."

Among the category of millionaires Phelps was referring to must be counted Henry J. Kaiser, who started his business career as a poor, sickly youth of 16, became an SMM, and was still vitally active in business and charitable pursuits well into his eighties. One of his lifelong guidelines: "Serve the public. Find projects that fill public needs. The more people who benefit, the better it is for you, too."

Kaiser carried his good works further than do most SMMs, because not only was he privately active in helping others, but many of his business ventures also served the public good. He built the Hoover and Bonneville Dams; during the Second World War he became a ship-builder, launching a vessel a day. His main fortune, however, was made as an aluminum producer.

When you reach the state of being an SMM, indulge yourself in the joy of helping others, not only in business projects designed for the public good, but in totally non-profit ventures into the world of financial good deeds. A common practice among SMMs is to set up foundations in their names to carry on their good deeds for them.

Either through a foundation that you establish or through independent donations, you may be in a position to provide your house of worship with the new edifice it has been needing, endow a new wing at the community hospital, build a new youth center, or provide scholarships for young men and women who show unusual promise.

Henry Kaiser was right in saying that the more people benefit from your good works, the more you will benefit, too. One of America's most successful merchants, Marshall Field, learned this long ago. His millions enabled Field to become a leader in philanthrophy.

Do you know what Field had to say about it? "Goodwill is the one and only asset that competition cannot undersell nor destroy."

So you really do benefit when you achieve the joy of helping others.

EXAMINE THESE MILLIONAIRES' LIFESTYLES

How do you want to live when you become a self-made millionaire? Those who have already achieved that status are a divided lot. Some live, as they say, in the lap of luxury. Others live almost as frugally as they did in the past.

But the wonderful thing about achieving wealth is that you have a choice! You can set your own lifestyle, frugal or luxurious though it may be.

The best way to learn the options open to you is to examine some of the lifestyles of today's SMMs.

Joe Hrudka: The man who made millions in the automotive gasket business lives in as much luxury as anyone might want. A three-million dollar mansion in Palm Springs; ownership of five dozen classic cars; employment of four household servants; providing his wife with more than a thousand dresses; a vacation home in Florida; regular jet trips to other areas; a life of retirement while still in his thirties; these are but a few of the luxuries Joe Hrudka provides for himself and his family.

Rich Dennis: This commodity trading wizard is worth in the neighborhood of $10-million, yet he still lives with his parents in their modest cottage, and ostentation is the furthest thing from his mind. He calls making money an intellectual challenge.

Percy Ross: This fur-trading millionaire loves to give lavish parties. For example, when he sold one of his companies, Ross staged a farewell for his employees—and gave six female workers mink coats. Another example: Always impressed by the polite and attentive manner of the skycaps at the Twin Cities Airport in Minneapolis, Ross recently decided to throw them a party. It was among the most lavish ever given at the airport's plush Decathlon Club. There were two bands, a folk singer, and a bevy of beautiful girls to serve as hostesses. Just Percy Ross' way of saying thank you. Oh yes, there was a full course dinner at which each skycap sat in a Hollywood director's chair with his name printed on the back, and each got to take the chair home with him.

Meshulam Riklis: You've met him several times in this book, and now it's time to learn how he lives. Riklis lives the way you'd expect a Manhattan millionaire to live. He lives in a mansion located off Fifth Avenue; he gets about in a chauffeur-driven limousine; he hobnobs with the other members of his financial class; he collects art. In other words, he lives in the elegant style that befits a multi-multi-multi-millionaire.

Many of the SMMs I've encountered have no desire for elegance or even luxury. Some live in tract houses, just as they did before achieving wealth. They may even drive the same beat-up old cars they've had for years.

Such people feel no need to show off their wealth. "After all, I know I'm rich," one of them told me, "and so do the people I associate with. So who needs a Rolls Royce to drive around town in?"

Some even enjoy looking inelegant. Youthful Wall Street millionaire Marc Howard enjoys the freedom of being able to walk into his downtown office dressed in blue jeans and a tee-shirt.

And that, of course, is what it's all about—freedom; freedom to set your own lifestyle, be it in elegance, living in a modest bungalow, or jetting off to the South of France several times a year; freedom to drive a Jaguar or a pickup truck; freedom to collect fine sculpture or plain old beer cans; freedom to indulge your whims, regardless of what they might be. It's an important reason for striving to become a self-made millionaire.

But wait. There's another reason, for many the most important reason of all. That's what we'll discuss next.

HOW TO MAKE MONEY-POWER WORK FOR YOU

If you were to take an informal survey of self-made millionaires, convincing them to respond with an absolutely honest answer, the great majority of them would admit that the real reason they worked so hard for all that wealth was the power that comes with it.

How do I know this? Because many of them have admitted it to me privately. And many of their associates have said it about them. They enjoy:

- Power over a thriving business organization
- Power and prestige in their communities
- Power in politics and government
- Power as leaders in their business field
- Power to see their orders put into instant action

The story is told of the time when John F. Kennedy went to visit President Eisenhower in the White House, as Kennedy was preparing to assume the presidency. Eisenhower started to tell Kennedy of the tremendous powers of the office, and to demonstrate his point he picked up the phone, spoke a few words, and within minutes a helicopter was landing on the White House lawn. Then the President gave the command for the helicopter to go back where it came from.

Now here was a man who had commanded millions of men in

the Second World War. His orders affected the destinies, the very lives, of the Allied fighting men. Few people had ever held as much power as he. And yet Dwight Eisenhower was greatly impressed by the fact that he was able to pick up the phone and summon a helicopter to the White House lawn. The craving of power is one of the strongest driving forces in men of great achievement.

One of the most effective means of obtaining power is to become wealthy. Most of the SMMs mentioned in this book would be able to do what Dwight Eisenhower was so proud of being able to do—pick up the phone and summon a chopper. In fact, that would seem small-time to most—a private jet is more like it.

But the power of wealth goes far beyond controlling the trappings of wealth; it involves leadership. As the self-made builder of a business fortune, you are a proven leader. And just as leaders crave power, the world cries out for leaders. Your leadership will be widely sought.

ENJOY NEWFOUND POWER AND PRESTIGE

"It began shortly after I'd made a success of my first business," John B. recalls. "I'd opened an office supply store followed by several nearby branches also selling office supplies. One day I got a call from the president of the local savings and loan. He wanted me to serve on the board of directors. Naturally, I was thrilled."

As time went on, John's business empire grew. There were more branches of his retail outlet, and he began leasing computers as a new venture. He had built quite a name for himself, and increasingly he was asked to lend that name to one project after another.

"I was elected chairman of the hospital fund drive and soon afterwards chairman of the hospital board itself. Then came the Youth League, regional office in various service clubs, etc."

Didn't all these extra activities hurt his business by taking him away from it?

"Not at all, In fact, they helped my business because I was being placed in close association with other businessmen—the very people who were prospective customers for what I was selling."

As John's computer service expanded into the big leagues, so did John.

"Along came invitations to serve on the boards of several nationally-known corporations. You don't have to guess the benefits I derived from all that."

The news media began to take notice as well. Speeches that John delivered to trade groups and business conventions were getting a lot of play in the press.

"What I had to say was making news. People were listening to me. Not just my own employees (I was accustomed to having my orders carried out) but the public at large, and especially other members of the business community. I had become, it seems, a man to be reckoned with."

John is obviously proud of his achievements—not only in becoming a millionaire several times over, but also in achieving a position of respect in his community, his profession, and in the business world at large.

If he had to make a choice, which would he give up—his wealth or his power and prestige?

John thinks for a moment before answering that question. "Well," he finally replies, "it would have to be the money. The power and prestige are worth a lot more to me."

And then he smiles. "But, of course, without the money there wouldn't be any power or prestige, would there?"

No, there probably wouldn't. It's one of the things that almost naturally accompanies substantial wealth.

YOU DON'T BUY POWER, YOU WIN IT

Don't get me wrong in what I've been saying. SMMs who are worth their salt don't throw their money around in an effort to obtain power and prestige. Only fools do that, because any prestige obtained in that manner is fleeting at best and illusory at worst.

If you don't buy power, then how do you get it? You win it. It's one of the prizes that goes along with having developed a proven business system. People respect those who have made it big on their own, and they seek out such people to provide them with leadership just as John B. was sought out by so many business and public service groups.

START USING MONEY-POWER RIGHT AWAY

You need not wait until you are fabulously wealthy in order to put money-power to work for you. To a lesser degree, it's available to you even at the starting stages of your empire-building process. And, while later you'll want to use this power for public-spirited endeavors, at first it should be applied toward the growth and expansion of your empire.

Here's what you can do:

- Join business and service groups to make contacts that will be profitable in your business.
- Convince your suppliers (those who count on you for buying their products and services) and your employees to work for community changes that will benefit your business.
- Join with other businessmen in working toward the area's growth and development, which naturally will benefit all members of the business community.
- Benefit from the publicity you get from accepting leadership roles in the organizations you join and the community projects you direct.

As the size of your business and your fortune grow, so will the levels at which your leadership is sought. Accept these responsibilities because they're an important part of the fortune-building process.

WHAT IT ALL BOILS DOWN TO

When all is said and done, the main point in working to become rich is pleasure, the pleasure of:

- Building a business empire from scratch
- Testing your business ideas
- Winning out over competition
- Overcoming obstacles
- Buying luxuries you couldn't afford before
- Being able to help others
- Living the lifestyle of your choosing

- Power and prestige that success brings

By following the lead of the SMMs in this book—learning from their mistakes and cashing in on the knowledge they've gained—you can enjoy any or all of the above pleasures. And, thanks to the proven methods of the SMMs as outlined here, you can skip many of the tribulations they've had to face en route.

ENJOY EVERY STEP OF THE WAY

Like many of the SMMs whose stories are related in this book, you can have a lot of fun from the first day you set your sights on millionairehood. I don't mean the carefree type of fun stemming from a trip to the beach or a county fair, I mean the fun of such things as:

- Charting your wealth-building course
- Developing a money mind
- Attracting wealth ideas
- Learning to use OPM
- Profiting from no-investment opportunities

Yes, for the SMM and the future SMM, these are exciting things. For the truly motivated, these are much of what life is all about. There's also a lot of fun in store for you as you:

- Multiply your money-making powers
- Read the signals that spell success
- Accumulate wealth-building formulas
- Creat "new twist" opportunities
- Speed up the flow of profits

ENJOY LEARNING THE SECRETS OF BUSINESS SUCCESS

"The tricks of the trade," they call them—and every trade has its tricks, the subtle things that spell the difference between money and really big money. Self-made millionaires gain particular pleasure in learning tricks such as these:

1. Work a business deal so you get in cheap but come out rich.
2. Make visualization convert profit dreams into profit realities.
3. Know in advance just how well you'll do.
4. Build personal contacts that attract riches.
5. Employ cost-cutting methods that at the same time increase profits.

And, as their empires grow and prosper, new pleasures await those who are approaching SMM status. They discover they are able to:

1. Make one venture breed many others.
2. Repeat their successes again and again.
3. Build a big name fast.
4. Expand nationally or even worldwide.
5. Snowball their profits through stock sales, franchising, and mergers.

To the man or woman who is made of the stuff SMMs are made of, all of these things are great fun. They comprise the challenges and the victories that make wealth-building so worthwhile.

The same type of intense pleasure awaits you as you chart your own wealth-building course and then carry it out. For each of the techniques I've been mentioning is carefully spelled out for you in the earlier chapters of this book. That's why you should plan on making this volume a steady companion. As you reach each new stage of your self-enrichment program, you have a ready guide to lead you through the increasingly fascinating process of multiplying your net worth.

JOIN THE MILLIONAIRE CROWD

Perhaps, a few years from now, I'll be writing a sequel to this book; by that time there should be thousands of new SMMs to write about. And do you know what I'm hoping? I'm hoping that by then I can include your success story.

There's no reason in the world why you can't be among the

new crop of self-made millionaires to emerge in the months and years ahead. In fact, it should be quite a bit easier for you than it was for those you've been reading about in this book. After all, they didn't have, set down on paper before them, the proven techniques that have built riches for others. You *do* have that advantage. So get busy!

And let me know of your success. I'd like very much to place your name in my file of self-made millionaires.

Index